Praise for
DETERMINED TO WIN

"Jean Driscoll is a role model, athlete, and true inspiration. *Determined to Win* is a touching and uplifting look into the life of a very special person and friend."

—JACKIE JOYNER KERSEE,
"Female Athlete of the Century," six-time Olympic medalist

"*Determined to Win* is a page-turner! I was immediately captivated by the external events of Jean's life experiences as well as the poignant strength of her inner person. This book is about so much more than being a winner of eight Boston Marathons. It inspires me to see what a real winner looks like. She looks like...acts like...Jean Driscoll."

—MARILYN MEBERG, *Women of Faith*

"The daily news is filled with the names and accomplishments of athletes in just about any sport imaginable. People who trained and developed bodies that cooperated and then worked through the doors of opportunity that life and accomplishment presented to them.

"But for Jean Driscoll every accomplishment, from the moment of birth to her eighth Boston Marathon trophy, was won only after overcoming discouragement, frustration, pain, and disappointment. She is living proof that the only limitations that can keep us down are in our hearts and minds.

"Jean's courage and determination will inspire you. Her spiritual freedom and physical accomplishments will challenge you to live more fully. This story is for everybody!"

—TERRY MEEUWSEN, *co-host,* The 700 Club

"From the very beginning, Jean provides the reader with a thrilling, first-person account of winning the B.A.A. Boston Marathon— the most prestigious and respected event in her sport. And then more important, she offers an equally open account of her remarkable life story. In the process, Jean demonstrates her perseverance, honesty, and triumph. As an unequaled eight-time winner of the Boston Marathon, she is widely accepted as an outstanding athlete and "first lady" of Boston. Her remarkably compelling and candid life story will motivate young and old alike."

—GUY MORSE, *executive director,*
Boston Athletic Association Boston Marathon

"Jean Driscoll is an extraordinary person with an extraordinary zest for life. Her impact as an athlete has been huge but pales in comparison to her greatness as a person. *Determined to Win* is about personal victory against all odds. Jean's "guts and gumption" plus her ever-growing faith in Christ encourage me greatly."

—TIM JOHNSON, *Illinois State Director,*
Fellowship of Christian Athletes

"Jean Driscoll's captivating autobiography has become the latest addition to our family's read-loud list. From her, we've learned lessons in compassion, understanding, determination, and hope. But we've also enjoyed the simple pleasure of reading a good book about an inspiring young woman's real-life adventures."

—JOY ZORN, *renowned family speaker*
and wife of Jim Zorn, Seattle Seahawks Pro Bowl quarterback

Dream BIG!

Jean Driscoll

John 17:4   2002

determined to

W I N

Dream BIG !

Gran Buscid

2002

John 17:4

determined to WIN

THE OVERCOMING SPIRIT *of*
Jean Driscoll
with JANET *and* GEOFF BENGE

SHAW BOOKS
an imprint of WATERBROOK PRESS

Determined to Win
A SHAW BOOK
PUBLISHED BY WATERBROOK PRESS
2375 Telstar Drive, Suite 160
Colorado Springs, Colorado 80920
A division of Random House, Inc.

ISBN 0-87788-192-8

Library of Congress Cataloging-in-Publication Data
Driscoll, Jean, 1966-
    Determined to win : the overcoming spirit of Jean Driscoll / Jean Driscoll with
Janet and Geoff Benge.
       p. cm.
    ISBN 0-87788-192-8 (pbk.)
    1. Driscoll, Jean, 1966- 2. Handicapped athletes—United States—Biography.
3. Spina bifida—Patients—United States—Biography. 4. Wheelchair sports—
United States. I. Benge, Janet, 1958- II. Benge, Geoff, 1954- III. Title.

GV697.D75 A34 2000
796.42—dc21
[B]

                                                                    00-055666

Printed in the United States of America
2001—First Trade Paperback Edition

10 9 8 7 6 5 4 3 2 1

To Mom, Dad, Frances, Ray, Ron, and Jacques
My life was built on the foundation that was laid in our home.
I love you all very much!

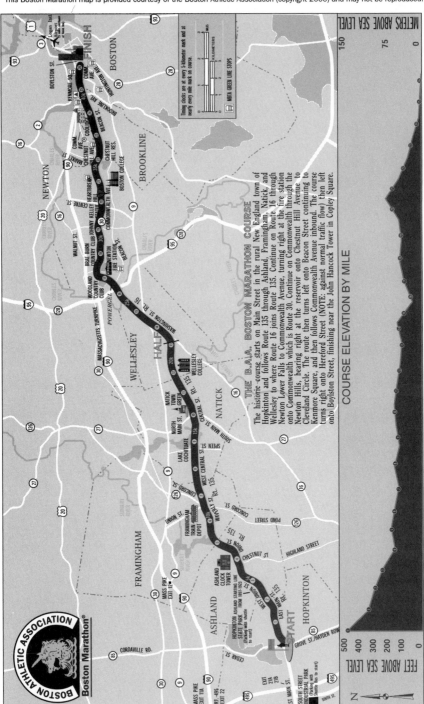

Map of the Boston Marathon

CONTENTS

Acknowledgments xi

Prologue: Determined to Win 1

1   A Little Island 5

2   Hard-Won Freedom 17

3   Poster Child 31

4   The Debacle 47

5   Life Sentence 61

6   Betrayed by My Body 75

7   The Coolest Thing I'd Ever Seen 89

8   New Direction 105

9   Illinois at Last 119

10   The Most Surreal Moment of My Life 133

11   All the Pieces Fitted Together 149

12   Winning Was in My Blood 167

13   Number Eight 181

Epilogue 199

Appendix: Milestones in My Life 201

ACKNOWLEDGMENTS

There are many people throughout my life who have contributed to who and where I am today. I am far from being a self-made woman. Whether I have been affected in major or minor ways doesn't matter; I have been affected. Unfortunately, it is not possible to name every individual who has had an impact on my life, so please forgive me if your name doesn't appear here. Time and space does not permit me to be as detailed as I could be. Suffice it to say that if I know you, you've probably had an effect on my life. Thank you.

Mom, Dad, Frances, Ray, Ron and Jacques: You didn't allow me to make excuses. My life with you was a training and proving ground for the incredible life I've led as an adult. Thank you!

Brad Hedrick: You gave me a chance to do things I never dreamed of doing. You believed in me enough to convince me to make the move that would change my life. Thank you!

Marty Morse: You developed potential in me I didn't know I had. You insisted that I become a stronger person with each passing year, both personally and athletically. Your presence in my life has been quite a blessing. Thank you!

Jim Derse: Without you, I don't know how I would have ever been able to compete at the elite level of sport. You were my first sponsor. You bought my first racing chair and first airplane ticket. I will never forget that. You were one of my earliest and biggest fans. Thank you!

Maryanna Young: You have vision far beyond what I can see. You do so much for me. You are one of the best agents/business partners/friends a girl could want to have. Thank you!

Ocean Spray, Litehouse, AccessLife.com, California Dates: You are my sponsors and I am so thankful for you. You support my habit…of training and racing. I couldn't enjoy success without you on my team. I love how you share the excitement of my victories and I appreciate your support immensely! Thank you!

Barry Ewing: You build the best sports chairs on the planet. I've never owned a racing chair that was not from Eagle Sportschairs. You have sponsored my equipment almost as long as I have been racing. You are family. Thank you!

The University of Illinois: You have shared the vision of Tim Nugent, one of the great pioneers in the wheelchair sports movement, for over fifty years. The university is known worldwide for its programs for students with disabilities. Thank you!

Tim Millikan, Craig Hampel, Maureen Gilbert, Phyllis Jones (and all the graduate assistants and volunteers): Your assistance is so valuable. Thank you!

Lori and Dan O'Brien, Debbie Richardson: You made Jesus real to me. Thank you!

Angie Duzynski, Cindy Leedale (and all my other nurse friends), Cindy (Owens) Housner, Don and Mikel Vandello, Cindy Griffin, Jim Ratzburg: You all knew me "when"—when I was struggling through life and doubting the possibility of a promising future. Your contributions in my life were significant, and your friendships helped push me forward when I was unsure of moving ahead. Thank you!

Don and Sue Otis: Your excitement about this book was contagious. It wouldn't have happened in as timely a manner without you. Thank you!

Janet and Geoff Benge: I am quite impressed by how efficiently you two work. You were respectful of my training/racing schedule yet still managed to conduct the necessary phone interviews, no matter what time zone I was visiting. Well done and "good on you!" Thank you!

Cara Kuhfal: Your research and outline paved the way for the direction of this book. Thank you!

Joan Guest: Your publishing experience and suggestions have enhanced the contents of this book. I've enjoyed your enthusiasm for this project. Thank you!

Derse Foundation: Without your help in underwriting some of the expenses associated with this book project, it would have been difficult to move forward as quickly as we did. Thank you!

Extended family and friends, Windsor Road Christian Church, Fellowship of Christian Athletes, Boston Athletic Association, Race Directors/Wheelchair Division Coordinators, Wheelchair Sports USA, Dr. Dustin and Rose Thomas, my teammates over the years, my host families, my fans, the Champaign-Urbana communities, the press/media, the endorsers of this book: Thank you! Thank you! Thank you!

Father God: I am saved by grace through faith. Thank you!

I Am the Baby

Jean Driscoll © 1999

Chorus:

I am the baby who lived.

I am the little one who received life as a gift.

I am the baby who lived.

I am the little one who received life as a gift.

I'm one in a thousand; I have spina bifida.

Pretty good odds, wouldn't you say?

Well, the fact of the matter is

my odds were not that good

when I came on my birthday.   (Chorus)

Some tend to argue that my life lacks quality.

Some say my future is dim.

Well, my legs are weak, but my heart is strong.

I have a voice and I belong.

They can't take my value away. (Chorus)

The Good Lord has blessed me with strength

beyond measure.

I cannot run, but I fly.

I am educated and I can vote.

I pay my taxes; it leaves me broke.

Life's not that different for me. (Chorus)

Just like my mother and father did,
I received life as a gift.
Just like my brothers and sister did,
I received life as a gift.
Just like my doctors and teachers did,
I received life as a gift.

I received life as a gift.
I received life as a gift.
I received life as a gift.
I received life as a gift.

Note: I wrote this song in the fall of 1999, and it came about as a result of several influences. First, I had a conversation with someone who referred to me as being "the baby who lived." (Her daughter died two weeks after being born with spina bifida.) I had never thought of myself in those terms before. Second, I was asked to be the keynote speaker for the 2000 National Spina Bifida Conference, and I wanted to do something special for it. Third, I attended a pro-life seminar that had a significant and lasting effect on me. Many babies are aborted because they are found through prenatal testing to have spina bifida.

In childhood I never dreamed I could be a world-class athlete.

DETERMINED TO WIN

Louise's yellow jersey bobbed up and down in front of me as we cruised at more than thirty miles per hour, down the hill past the fifteen-mile mark. Determined not to let her get away from me, I punched the wheels with all my might, trying to squeeze out every last bit of speed I could. The road was rough, and as I sped along, *wham!* My racing wheelchair hit a hidden pothole, sending it and me flying into the air. I held my breath as I sailed forward and slammed down hard on all three wheels. I tapped my brakes to regain control. It all happened in a split second, but that was all the opportunity Louise needed. I looked up and she had pulled away from me.

I pumped my arms still faster. I had to catch her quickly. If I let her get away from me, I knew I wouldn't see her again until the finish line.

Steadily, with each punch of the wheels, I gained on her until I felt myself slip back into her draft.

We raced on together until Heartbreak Hill—a two-mile long test of endurance. *It's now or never,* I told myself. *It's time to make a break. This is the last big hill in the race, and hills are my strength!* I tucked my head down into the wind and dug into my pushrims as hard as I could.

As I began to climb, Louise swung out of my draft and tried to pull level with me. I could see her front wheel in my peripheral vision. Determined not to let her beat me to the top, I kept pushing. About halfway up the grueling climb her wheel disappeared. I turned my head. Louise was about twenty meters behind me, stroking hard and fast. I redoubled my efforts. My stomach and back muscles screamed with pain, but I ignored them. I had to increase the gap between us to have any chance of winning.

I had the lead as I crested the hill and passed Boston College. But the powerful Australian was still behind me as I rounded Cleveland Circle onto Beacon Street. *Keep going, Jean. Keep going!* I urged myself forward. *If you let up one bit, she'll catch you.*

By the time I got to the bridge at mile twenty-four, I was still ahead. But from here the course flattened out. This would give Louise the advantage. She raced well downhill and on the flat.

I kept the lead. But with a mile and a half to go, I caught sight of Louise when I turned to see how far ahead I was. She was barreling down Beacon Street. I'd been taking a break (coasting for a second or two to get rid of the lactic acid that causes muscles to "burn") after every twenty strokes, but I knew I couldn't do that again. I stroked two hundred times in a row, forcing my wheels forward. Stroke…stroke…stroke. I had to keep Louise at bay.

I turned onto Hereford. Louise wasn't right behind me, but I knew she couldn't be far away. I straightened my chair after rounding the corner. As I did so, my right back wheel hit a manhole cover, causing my chair to wobble. I heard a collective gasp go up from the crowd. Quickly, I regained control of my chair and kept pounding. The end was in sight now. I could see the finish line. But I couldn't let up. Louise had beaten me before when I had been in sight of the finish line. Adrenaline surged through me. I raced forward with every ounce of strength I had, refusing to relax until I felt the tape welcome me as I broke through it at the finish line.

The crowd roared. Twenty feet...ten...five...the public address announcer yelled, "Number Eight! She's done it! Jean Driscoll, eight-time winner of the Boston Marathon!" I felt the tape snap across my chest and raised my arms in exhilaration. I had done it. I was the first athlete ever to win eight Boston Marathons!

Yet as I sat there at the end of the race, amid the cheering of the crowd and in the glare of the national media lights, there was a surreal quality about it all. Anyone who knew me in grade school and high school would have been hard-pressed to believe it. How could Jean Driscoll, the little girl with the therapeutic shoes and leg braces, and later the wheelchair, have become the first person to win eight Boston Marathons in any category? I'd come a long way from those years growing up in Milwaukee...

Top: The Driscoll kids, Christmas 1969 (from left): me, Ray, Ron, and Francie. Jacques was not yet born.

Bottom: My first-grade school photo, 1972.

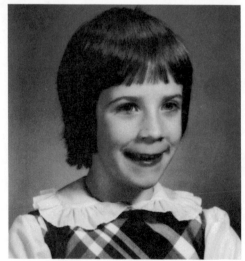

ONE

A Little Island

"Jean! Jean! Get down here now!" My mother's voice reverberated up the stairs of our small Milwaukee home.

"Coming," I yelled back, giving my dark blond hair a final tug with the brush. I pulled up my green plaid polyester pants—hand-me-downs from my older sister, Francie, that I hadn't quite grown into—and walked out of our bedroom in the converted attic of our bungalow to the edge of the stairs.

"I'm putting the twins in the car," I heard my mother call up to me again. This was followed by the sound of my three-and-a-half-year-old twin brothers, Ray and Ron, scampering across the kitchen floor with her at their heels. I sat down on my behind, locked my knees, and launched myself from the top step in much the same way Francie went down the slide at the park. Plop, plop, plop. I bounced down all thirteen steps in record time.

At the bottom I scrambled to my feet, adjusted the right strap on my lower leg brace and headed for the door. As I walked, I could hear the inside of my therapeutic brown leather shoes scraping against the tile floor. Ever since I'd learned to walk at age two, I'd walked on the inside of my feet and ankles in an attempt to keep my balance. The metal hinges that attached my shoes to the braces squeaked loudly. Unlike my three siblings, I could never sneak up on anyone.

I opened the passenger-side door of our two-door Torrino. Glancing at the twins who were already climbing over each other in the backseat, I plunked myself down onto the vinyl seat and swung in my legs. My mother was already wedged into the driver's seat, her maternity dress billowing around the steering wheel. A brown paper bag lay between us. I knew what it contained: several pairs of underwear. Because I had little warning when I needed the bathroom, Mom had already alerted the teacher she would be bringing along some extra undies for me.

———

The metal hinges that attached my shoes to the braces squeaked loudly.

———

"You boys sit still now," commanded my mother as she pulled onto Fifty-fifth Street.

Five minutes later we were at the entrance to Hampton Public School. Francie, who was a year older than I, had already transferred from here to Mother of Perpetual Help, the local parish school. I would also be transferring there when I reached first grade. But for now, this low, brown brick building was the object of my dreams. I was only four years old. My birthday was still two months away, in November, but I was as ready as anyone for kindergarten. I had studied all the pictures Francie had brought home, quizzed her incessantly about the playground rules, and learned the words to the alphabet song by heart. That determination to succeed eventually became a hallmark for me, but at that age it was just my means of survival.

"Come on, Jean," chided Ray, looking back at me. I stopped staring at the school and began making my way toward the main doors. Mom was already there, the paper bag of underwear tucked under her left arm, each of her hands holding one twin in a vise-like grip. I followed her through the back door and down a painted cinderblock corridor to Room 4. She knocked lightly on the door and opened it. I took a deep breath and glared at Ron and Ray, silently reminding them they had better not do anything to embarrass me, now that I was a real schoolgirl. The two of them grinned back in unison. Even though they weren't identical, they both had the same impish smile.

I stepped into the classroom. It was just as Francie had described it. There was a large green square carpet on the floor with a group of children sitting cross-legged on it. Under the window was a long bookshelf, and on the front wall was a huge chalkboard.

"Welcome," said a kind voice. I looked up and there was Mrs. Kagelmann, her teased brown hair piled on top of her head. "Come on in and find yourself somewhere to sit, Jean," she said.

Hesitantly, I took a step toward the mat, nearly losing my balance as I did so. Out of the corner of my eye I saw a little girl nudge her neighbor. Two boys whispered to each other. I headed for a spot near the back, but as I dragged my feet nearer, the other children quickly scooted away from the area. I could feel my face getting hot. I sat down quickly while the two girls nearest me wiggled farther away until there was no one within arm's reach.

A minute later my mother and brothers were gone, and I was

alone in a room filled with strangers. I sat quietly as Mrs. Kagelmann resumed reading *Curious George*. I couldn't concentrate on
the words, though, as my mind was reeling. Part of me had always
known I was different. After all, I had a spongy lump on my lower
back, I could stick a pin in my feet and feel no pain, and I wobbled
from side to side when I walked, looking a lot like Charlie Chaplin.
Despite this, everywhere I had been up to this point—be it my
grandma's house, my cousin Sandy's home, or church—I always
felt like I belonged. Now here I was, alone with my leg braces and
brown paper bag, a little island in a sea of children who looked at
me as though I came from another planet.

**Now here I was, a little island in a sea of
children who looked at me as though I
came from another planet.**

I had a vague idea of how I was different. My father would
sometimes hoist me onto his lap and show me medical diagrams of
spina bifida from my mother's old nursing books. He would then
try to explain to me that this was what I had, and that one in one
thousand babies were born with the condition.

Spina bifida is the most common type of neural tube defect,
one that affects the spinal cord and its protective coverings. In this
case, the spine does not close properly during growth in the first
month of life in the womb. The spinal cord may then protrude
through the back, causing damage that results in varying degrees of
paralysis.

When I was a child there was little treatment for spina bifida and no prevention. Now research shows that taking folic acid during pregnancy can help prevent the condition as the baby forms, and ongoing research is being conducted with the goal of correcting the condition even before birth! My knowing the Latin name of my condition, however, wasn't much comfort in that classroom. I would have given anything to be "normal" and have the other children like me.

During that first day in kindergarten, I talked to Mrs. Kagelmann several times but not to any of the other children. However, when Mom picked me up after school, I was still optimistic. The joy of being a schoolgirl outweighed the negative reactions of my classmates. I looked forward to getting home and having Dad ask me what I'd learned at school that day, just as he always asked Francie.

That night, I learned that new responsibilities came with being a schoolgirl. I began helping with the dishes. Francie and I would drag our chairs over from the kitchen table and kneel on them in front of the sink. We took turns washing and drying on a weekly basis. Mom also told me I was expected to rinse out in the toilet the cloth diapers I wore each night. They, along with any wet sheets, were to be left soaking in the laundry tub beside the wringer washing machine in the basement in the morning. Getting down to the basement was a breeze, but climbing up the stairs took a little more effort.

By the time my fifth birthday rolled around on November 18, 1971, Mrs. Kagelmann had helped break the ice with the other students. I was now a bona fide member of the class. I even had a best friend, Lisa Warner. We shared scissors and secrets and helped each other with jigsaw puzzles, just as any friends would. However, unlike the other kids, I was always nervous, aware that in less than a second my world could change. In an instant, I could go from cozily chatting to Lisa and coloring in pictures to making a frantic dash for the bathroom. Sometimes I made it, and sometimes I didn't. On the latter occasions, I often left a telltale trail partway down the hallway. Yet despite these occasional embarrassing episodes, I loved school.

Three weeks after Christmas recess ended, my baby brother, Jacques, was born. Mom brought him home from the hospital the next day, and Dad set his crib up in their bedroom. Even at five years of age, I could see that our three-bedroom, one-bathroom, Cape Cod–style house was being stretched to capacity.

Within weeks my mother was back to work as a nurse in a nursing home from 3:30 in the afternoon till 11:30 at night. When Mom left for work, Lil, a friend of hers, would take care of us until my father came home. One afternoon while I was sitting on the piano bench in the living room eating a snack, I heard my mother and Lil talking.

"I don't know how you're going to keep up with things and work as hard as you do, Angie, especially now that you have the baby. Thank goodness he's healthy at least," Lil said in a hushed voice that I wasn't supposed to hear.

"He sure is," my mother affirmed. I felt the sting of comparison, though all Mom was doing was expressing gratitude for Jacques's good health.

"You have to take care of yourself and get more rest," chided her friend. "Five children and a full-time evening job just don't go together."

Mom laughed wearily. "That's not going to happen anytime soon. Jean could keep me busy all by herself. She seems to need to see a different specialist every week or two. The urologist just put her on a course of antibiotics to control her bladder infections. Let's hope it does the job. The pills aren't cheap." She put down the sock she was darning. "And Jim had to send in his license last week, so now I'm responsible for all the driving."

"Really?!" gasped Lil. "I thought his epilepsy was under control."

"It's not too bad," replied Mom. "He hasn't had an all-out seizure for quite a while, but he has a lot of auras. A couple of weeks ago when he was out driving, he blacked out for a second and veered off the road."

"Oh my."

"It wasn't that bad, really. He regained consciousness quickly and got things back under control. But it gave him a scare. And now it's pretty depressing for him to have to send in his license. His work isn't going so well, either. He never knows which part of the factory he'll be working in until he gets there."

Lil reached out and patted my mother's hand. "It won't always be like this," she said reassuringly.

I heard my mother sigh. "I just wish there were more hours in the day and that I wasn't tired all the time," she said.

As I walked to the kitchen to get a glass of water, Mom noticed my shoes. She turned toward me, looking down at my feet as she often did. "Jean, come here and sit down," she said, pointing to the patch of floor by her feet.

I made my way over to her and sat down. As my mother started to examine the soles of my shoes, I looked away guiltily.

"I thought I told you to stay off the cement!" she exclaimed.

"I only wanted to throw the basketball into the hoop," I said, my stomach turning into a knot. Sports had always attracted me.

My mother held up my left leg so Lil could see it. "Each time we have to get these shoes resoled, it costs twelve dollars." Her brown eyes bored into mine. "That's two hours' pay, Jean. I have to work for two whole hours when you don't do what you're told. From now on, you only walk on the grass, do you hear me?"

She lifted up the other leg to check the brace. "This girl!" she exclaimed. "If she gets on the pavement, she can wear those soles right through in a couple of hours. And she's nearly worn through the metal on the braces again." Mom looked at me, exhaustion and worry showing in her frustration and her tone of voice. "Welding isn't free, either."

I didn't want to be reminded that I cost my mother money we did not have.

I sat captive in my mother's gaze, waiting for the conversation to change course. Fortunately for me, Ron came racing into the room with a splinter in his hand, and I was allowed to go. I quickly fled upstairs to my room.

I threw myself on the bed, hot tears stinging my eyes. I didn't want to be reminded that I cost my mother money we did not have and that my father often had to work overtime to pay my medical bills or to resole the shoes I hated wearing anyway.

If only I was like Francie, I told myself. Francie wore cool black-and-white saddle shoes. In the morning her mattress was dry. And her legs were strong, so she could run around the neighborhood, skip rope in the driveway, and jump down the stairs two at a time. But no matter how much I wanted to be like Francie, I wasn't, and I knew I never would be.

The following fall, I joined Francie at Mother of Perpetual Help School, or MPH as I quickly learned to abbreviate it. I could see the school from our front yard, but because of the wear and tear on my shoes and the pain I got in my back and legs when I tried to walk distances, there was no way I could get myself there. For the first year my mother arranged for a van service to pick me up, but the driver was constantly late and this caused a lot of stress in our family's already chaotic morning schedule. By the second year, Mom had had enough. She decided Francie should take me to school in the red wagon we kept in the garage.

"Come on. Get in," said Francie with resignation the first morning she took me.

I glared back. I didn't want to get into the wagon any more than she wanted to push me in it, but we had no choice. When Mom said something, we did it, so I climbed in and settled my schoolbag between my legs.

"I'll push, you steer," instructed Francie.

I grabbed the black handle and held it steady. "Okay," I said.

I felt Francie's hands on my back as she shoved me down the driveway and onto the sidewalk. "This is a pain," she said loudly, and I knew she was referring to more than just having to push me to school. She made it clear that I was often a nuisance. No child would have liked the wet-bed smell in the bedroom we shared or the way my Great Aunt Florence had brought two bags filled with Barbie doll clothes for me when she came to visit—and nothing for anyone else. Francie and the twins also taunted me about being Dad's favorite, though that had few advantages as far as I could see. From their youthful sibling perspectives, I took up a lot of time and received way too much attention.

The red wagon bumped along, and within minutes we were at school. Francie abandoned me at the beginning of the bike racks, leaving me to climb out of the wagon and park it behind the rack. I then dragged my feet and the heavy braces one by one up the twenty-two steps that led into school. "Great," I heard a sarcastic voice behind me say. "We're stuck behind *her* again."

I felt my face turn as red as the wagon I had just ridden in, but I never looked around. I hated all of the stairs at MPH. The kids behind me always had to wait, and even when they weren't rude enough to say something, I could feel their stares burrowing into my back.

After reaching the top of the steps, I had to walk past one class-room to get to mine. Once I made it, I was rewarded with a place to sit down. I was painfully aware that I got to school in a very undig-nified manner, but at least after I got there, I was able to get around on my own. This was something I valued greatly. I had no idea, though, just how fragile this hard-won independence really was.

Top: The Driscoll kids in 1972 (from left): me, Ray, Francie (in back), baby Jacques, and Ron.

Bottom: This is how I walked from age two to age fourteen.

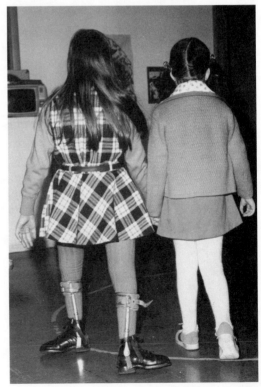

TWO

Hard-Won Freedom

"Stop the ball," David Stolpa yelled urgently, flailing his arms.

I looked around to see it speeding along the blacktop playground toward me. Taking a deep breath I lunged at it, wanting more than anything to be the hero of our third-grade game of dodge ball. Keeping my eye on the ball, I stuck out my right foot to deflect it. I felt the ball go under my foot and then heard a sickening crack. I fell to the ground, convinced that I had broken one of the metal rods on my leg brace.

Mrs. Wimmer, our PE teacher, rushed over to me. "Are you okay, Jean?" she asked, kneeling down beside me. By now my leg was starting to swell.

"Linda!" Mrs. Wimmer yelled. She looked around for my friend, one of the fastest runners in the class. "Go and get Jean's wagon. We need to get her into the office. "

Two minutes later, Linda raced back with the wagon in tow, and I was lifted into it. Mrs. Wimmer then pulled me to the nurse's office. My arrival caused a flurry of activity. Sister Rafael, principal of the school, came in to see what the problem was and immediately called my mother. It was nearly the end of the school day, and my sister, Francie, was summoned to the office. Francie's job was to take me home, going over as few bumps as possible, so my mother could take a look at me and decide what should be done next.

The wagon ride home was excruciatingly painful, even though Francie did her best not to jar me. The worried look on her face heightened my own sense of panic about what I had done. I wasn't accustomed to sympathy from my siblings.

Keeping my eye on the ball, I stuck out my right foot to deflect it and then heard a sickening crack.

When I got home my mother took one look at my now very swollen leg and called Dr. Flatley, my orthopedic surgeon. He wasn't available, but Mom explained to his nurse what had happened and asked if the doctor could meet us at the emergency room. The nurse promised to call back as soon as she could make the arrangements. While I waited, I lay on the couch, my leg throbbing with pain.

The minutes ticked by and the pain in my leg intensified. Finally the phone rang. Mom rushed to answer it. After she hung up, she swung into action. "Francie," she yelled, "I need your help."

Francie popped her head around the corner of the kitchen. "What?"

"I have to take Jean to the emergency room. I need you to watch the twins and Jacques."

"Okay, Mom." My sister's tone was unusually cooperative. She often resented helping out, but that afternoon everyone was focused on my accident.

During the trip to the hospital, the only thing I could think about was the shot I was bound to get. Needles petrified me. When I saw them coming, I usually started crying, no matter how my mother had tried to bribe me ahead of time.

Despite my ongoing medical problems, this was the first trip I could remember taking to the hospital. I knew from what Mom had told me that I was whisked away for exploratory surgery within moments of my birth. It was twelve hours before she saw me again. My parents were told there was nothing the doctors could do for me, but I was kept in the hospital for observation for a week and a half anyway. Mom liked to tell people that after I finally came home, she found out just how "observant" this observation had been. Although she did everything she could think of to get me to drink properly, the milk I drank bubbled back through my nose, making me gasp for air. Finally, in frustration, she opened my mouth widely and discovered to her dismay that I had a hole about the size of a quarter in the roof of my mouth. I had a cleft palate! So it was back to the hospital again.

Since then most of my medical trips had been visits to the offices of a never-ending array of specialists. I had a pediatrician, a neurologist, a urologist, and a number of other "ologists" that I could not name. But despite these frequent visits, I had avoided having to go back to hospital—until now.

Mom dropped me off at the emergency entrance of Milwaukee Children's Hospital. I was offered a wheelchair and waited in the hospital lobby until Mom parked the car in the parking garage and came back for me.

One advantage of my mother's being a nurse was that she

knew who the best specialists were in the area. She allowed the on-call doctor to take x-rays of my leg, but she insisted on waiting for Dr. Flatley to do whatever it was he felt needed to be done.

It was six o'clock before the doctor finally arrived. I was hungry and tired by the time I was wheeled into one of the small examination rooms and lifted onto an examination bed. My eyes were drawn immediately to the metal tray in the corner with the syringes and small plastic bottles on it. As it happened, I had nothing to fear in regard to shots. I was about to find out that while my doctor had a wonderful reputation with bones, he seemed to have no idea that I had a lot of feeling in the fronts and sides of my legs.

**The doctor seemed to have no idea that
I had a lot of feeling in my legs.**

"It's broken about halfway down the right tibia," he said to my mother, holding up one of my x-rays for her to see.

With one more glance at the x-ray, Dr. Flatley turned to me and picked up my broken leg. I let out a howl of pain, but he didn't stop. He twisted my leg about thirty degrees. I began sobbing from the pain and imploring my mother to help me. She held me down firmly while Dr. Flatley manipulated my bones back into place.

When he was satisfied with his work, the doctor started to wrap my leg in a cloth stocking, the first stage of a cast. I tried to focus on the upside of having a leg cast to take my mind off the ordeal I had just endured. Having a cast would be cool, I told myself. I had often envied other kids at school who had broken a bone. Having a cast looked like fun; everyone got to write neat things on it.

I soon discovered that this was the only good thing about having a cast. My skin itched incessantly under it, and the normal tasks I struggled with—like getting to the bathroom on time, keeping my balance when I stood still, and taking a bath—were all made much more difficult by the cast.

School was worst of all. Dr. Flatley and my mother had discussed the ease with which I could rebreak my tibia, especially now that I was getting around on crutches with a heavy cast on one leg. So the thing I hated most happened: Special arrangements were made for me. Two of my friends, Kim and Dawn, were designated to be my helpers. They took turns pulling me in the red wagon across the long open area that connected the east and west wings of the school. Then, with the wagon's wheels squeaking on the tile floor, they would wheel me past the principal's office and down the hall to the "big kids" bathroom. The two girls also took turns sitting with me in the classroom during lunch break and recess, since there was no way I could negotiate the thirty steps down to the lunchroom.

Finally, after six long and very inconvenient weeks, it was time to go back to Children's Hospital for a checkup. All the way up Interstate 43 I nagged my mother, asking her what the doctor was going to do to me. I had often relived the horror of the original bone manipulations, done without any anesthetic, and I was terrified by the thought there might be more of the same ahead for me.

At the hospital, it seemed that my worst fears were realized. I listened while Dr. Flatley told my mom that the bone was not healing properly, and that the only option was to rebreak it and reset it in a slightly different position. This, however, could not be done the same day, and I had twenty-four hours to torment myself with what lay ahead. The following day I was admitted to the hospital. Fortunately, rebreaking a leg somehow warranted more pain management than setting one, and I was anesthetized while the operation was performed.

All in all, it was twelve weeks before the cast was finally taken off for good. With it gone, my leg felt weird and floppy, and I couldn't put any weight on it. I was determined, though, to get back to walking and getting around on my own. Each day I tried to walk a step or two without the aid of crutches, and as the weeks went by I slowly regained strength in my leg.

I recovered just in time for a new adventure.

I recovered just in time for a new adventure: Camp Wawbeek. In July 1975, Mom drove me 125 miles to a summer camp in Wisconsin Dells sponsored by the Easter Seals Society. As we got closer to our destination, troubling thoughts invaded my eight-year-old mind. What if no one liked me? How would I know what I was supposed to do? Where was I going to sleep? By the time we pulled into the winding, dirt driveway that led to the camp, I was so nervous I could barely talk.

Mom climbed out of the car. "Well, here we are. Let's go. Doesn't this look great?"

I nodded cautiously and followed her around to the trunk to get my bags. As we gathered my things, a college-age girl with long blond pigtails bounced up to us, clipboard in hand. "Hi," she greeted us.

I stepped behind my mother, peeking around her.

"What's your name?" the girl asked me.

I clamped my mouth shut as Mom's hands gently propelled me from my hiding place.

"I'm Mrs. Driscoll, and this is my daughter Jean," said mom. "Where would you like us to go?"

"I'm Sandy," replied the girl. She studied her clipboard. "Let me see, Jean Driscoll...you're in Tomahawk. It's that bunkhouse over there." She pointed to a long building with a low veranda in front and a bright red door. "Let me help you with your bags. Then I'll take you down to the Trading Post to put some money on your account. She smiled down at me.

I tried to smile back, but my lips wouldn't cooperate. I had never been on my own in such unfamiliar surroundings before, and I knew my mom would soon leave.

As Mom and Sandy walked down the concrete sidewalk, I followed along on the grass. As we walked, I noticed something very unusual. There were no stairs. All the buildings had ramps at the entrances or were flush with the ground; none had stairs.

An hour later my mother had taken care of all the arrangements, and I stood and watched as she drove away.

"Anyone for Kool-Aid and cookies?" I heard a voice offer.

I turned around to see a cart being wheeled out of a large building marked "Dining Room." I suddenly realized I was hungry and began making my way toward it. Several other kids were headed in that direction too. One boy was on crutches, and another had the same telltale gait I did. A few minutes later, as I sat on a tree stump drinking a cup of cherry Kool-Aid, I took a good look around. Cars and vans continued to roll up. Some of the vans had elaborate wheelchair lifts on their side doors, and many of the cars had special wheelchair racks on the back. Shocked, I realized most of the children being helped out of these vehicles were a lot worse off than I was. Some of them couldn't walk at all or even hold their heads up straight.

As the two-week camp progressed, my shyness slipped away. For the first time in my life I was surrounded by people who were less able than I was. I could make it to the bathroom on a good day; many of the other children had to wear diapers all the time or were catheterized. I was capable of telling anyone what I wanted; others had slurred speech. I could feed myself just fine; some of the

---

While we were having a cookout, I overheard the counselor from the next bunkhouse talking to my counselor.

---

others had deformed or unresponsive hands and arms. I soon found myself helping these other kids eat, pushing their wheelchairs, and participating in sports events. Seeing life from the perspective of a winner was a new experience for me. But as much as I loved it, I knew it wouldn't last. Eventually the camp would end.

One night, while we were having a cookout, I overheard the counselor from the next bunkhouse talking to Sandy, my counselor. "Have you noticed what a good little helper Jean is?" she said.

"Yeah, she's great," replied Sandy. "Jean is a natural leader, that's for sure."

I stopped chewing my hamburger, stunned by her words. Was

Sandy really talking about me, Jean Driscoll? The same Jean Driscoll who had to be pushed to school in a red wagon by an unwilling sister? The same Jean Driscoll who hobbled slowly up the stairs, making the students behind her late for class? I was a natural leader? If it was true, and I had my doubts, it could be so only here at an Easter Seals camp and not in the real world. Yet a tiny seed of confidence was planted in my heart at that moment.

Some of the confidence I gained at Camp Wawbeek did follow me home. One Friday night the following spring, my friend Marcia leaped up the back stairs to our house and rang the doorbell to be let in. "I can ride a two-wheeled bike now," she announced, her big eyes gleaming with excitement.

"What?" I put the last of the silverware onto the dish rack and wiped my sudsy hands on my pants.

"I can ride my bike without the training wheels! "

"No way!" I exclaimed.

"Come on," Marcia said as I climbed off the stool, her excitement urging me toward the door. "Just watch." She jumped off the stoop and grabbed her bike.

"Look at me, Jean! No training wheels! "

As Marcia rode down the driveway, I stared after her, the cogs turning in my brain. Marcia was seven years old, a full two years younger than I was, and she could now ride a two-wheeler. I, on the other hand, still relied heavily on my training wheels. This was humiliating. I couldn't go over the curb or around corners fast. Indignation suddenly surged through me.

"I'm going to learn too!" I yelled back. "I can do it if you can!"

As soon as I stood beside Marcia's bike, I knew it wasn't going to work. Marcia was taller than me, and there was no way I was going to be able to touch the ground with my feet flat. Since I couldn't stand on tiptoes because of the paralysis of my legs, I needed a smaller bike on which to practice riding without training wheels: one smaller than Marcia's or my own. I frowned.

"Jean, come and finish the dishes," yelled my mother.

"I have to go," I told Marcia and climbed back up the stairs. During the rest of the evening, I worried about how I was going to catch up with my friend and learn to ride a two-wheeler.

The next morning I drifted over to Marcia's house to play. There I saw her five-year-old brother Ricky's bike leaning against a tree.

"I bet I could ride that!" I exclaimed. I climbed onto the tiny bike. "I can touch the ground with my feet!"

For the first hour, Marcia stayed in her yard with me. She rode around in circles, encouraging me to keep trying to lift my feet off the ground and onto the pedals. It was slow going, though. With the limited strength I had in my legs and feet, I hadn't developed a good sense of balance. The bike wobbled over on me time after time.

"I'm going inside now," Marcia finally said, obviously bored with my progress. "But you can stay out here with the bike if you want. Just leave it by the garage when you're done."

When Marcia left, I got back on the bicycle and tried again. The bike teetered many times and keeled over on me a few, but I managed to avoid hitting the pavement too hard. The bike was so small, I could usually get my feet to the ground in time.

By lunchtime, when Marcia's mother invited me in for a sandwich, I could ride past two houses without falling off. By three o'clock, the time when the paperboy delivered the *Milwaukee Journal*, I was staying on the bike for four houses. Still I pressed on. My goal was to be free to ride as far as I wanted, just like Marcia. Finally, I counted seven, eight, nine, ten houses in a row. Exhilaration swept over me. I was really riding a two-wheeled bike without training wheels!

It was suppertime when I turned the bike around and headed for my house. I burst into the kitchen. "Mom," I yelled, "I can ride a two-wheeler. Come and watch me!"

I was really riding a two-wheeled bike!

My mother got up from scrubbing the kitchen floor. "What do you mean?" she frowned.

"Come on," I urged enthusiastically, heading out the door.

As I picked up Ricky's bike my mother called to me, cutting through my euphoria. "Jean, don't get on that thing. You'll break your neck!"

"No, I won't, Mom. Honest. Just watch me," I replied, panicked by the thought that my mother might forbid me from enjoying this hard-won freedom. "Look, I can touch the ground if I have to." I sat on the bike and demonstrated how my feet touched the ground on both sides.

My mother sighed deeply. "Well, just around the driveway," she said, resignation etched in her voice. "And be careful."

I sat down on the seat and pushed off with my feet. My heart pounded with pride as I maneuvered my way around the driveway three times. "See! See! I'm riding a two-wheeler. I'm doing it!" I shouted.

"Well, I guess you can," agreed my mother. "Dad should be home soon. Maybe he'll take the training wheels off your bike for you. But don't go out in the street.

I returned Ricky's bike, riding along the sidewalk and being careful not to veer into the street.

An hour after I arrived back home, my father strolled up the driveway. I scooted to the door to wait for him. "Dad! I can ride a two-wheeled bike without training wheels," I exclaimed, not even waiting for him to put down his lunchbox.

"How did you learn to do that?" he asked.

"Marcia helped me, and I learned on Ricky's bike," I replied. "Can you take the training wheels off my bike?"

He smiled down at me. "Let's get a wrench."

A huge grin spread across my face as my father loosened the bolts that secured the training wheels to my bike. The bicycle was blue with a white banana seat and curly handlebars, and I laughed at how cool I would look riding it without the babyish training wheels.

Finally, the extra wheels were lying discarded on the grass. My father put his wrench back in the toolbox. "I bet you can ride this around the block," he said, lifting the bike up and handing it to me.

"Yep," I said, eager to prove myself. "I bet I can."

"Come on, let's go." He grabbed his bike.

I climbed on my own bicycle minus its training wheels for the first time. Carefully, I put one leg on the pedal while the other leg was on the ground, then struggled to regain my balance. It took at least a minute, but my father waited patiently. Finally, the conditions were right to push off. I scooted my right foot along the ground, then lifted it over and onto the other pedal. I was riding!

Together Dad and I rode down Villard Street to the corner of Fifty-sixth Street and back again. In actual distance we rode about half a mile, but when measured in terms of my newly discovered freedom, I felt as though I had been to the moon and back.

Terry Meeuwsen and me (on the right) at an Easter Seals Society benefit luncheon. Erin Connolly was the other poster child that year.

THREE

POSTER CHILD

Shyly I glanced around the group of people gathered on the sidewalk outside Pius XI High School. "Don't forget your manners now that you're a poster child," Mom said, guiding me toward two of the officials who were shaking hands at the door.

I smiled on the inside. This was all proving to be one big adventure for me. In January 1976, midway through my fourth-grade year, I had been invited to become a poster child for the Milwaukee branch of the Easter Seals Society. Seven-year-old Erin Connolly, who was developmentally disabled, had been invited to be a poster child along with me.

I was following closely behind my mother when I spotted a woman getting out of the car behind us. The glamorous brunette walked straight up to me and reached out her hand. "Hi," she said with a gleaming smile. "I'm Terry Meeuwsen, and you must be Jean Driscoll. I'm so glad to meet you."

I knew I should say something, but I just stood there, too shy and overawed by how pretty she was to respond. In front of me stood the woman who had been Miss America three years before, in 1973. My mother had told me Terry Meeuwsen was a celebrity spokesperson for the Easter Seals Society. In fact, that was what brought the three of us together. Erin, Terry, and I were going to make an appearance at the All Stars Tournament fund-raising event at a local high school.

"Come on, girls, hold hands for the photo," coaxed a photographer from the newspaper. I was nine years old and felt I was a little too old to be holding hands with other girls, but reluctantly I reached out and took Erin's hand. Lights flashed in our eyes.

"Hop in the photo, Terry," yelled the photographer.

Terry Meeuwsen hurried over.

"Now, you two girls, put one arm around Terry and smile for me," directed the photographer.

A man in a suit came up to us. He shook hands with Terry and patted my head. "Here," he said, pulling two identical red sweatshirts from a plastic bag. "Put these on, kids."

I took the sweatshirt and pulled it over my head. It had the official Easter Seals logo, the outline of an Easter lily, on the front. Looking at the back of Erin's shirt I could see it had four stars with the words "All Stars" emblazoned across the back.

"You two look great," said the man with a chuckle. "And you have plenty of room to grow into them!"

I looked down. The bottom came nearly to my knees, but I was glad to have a new sweatshirt of my own. The matching shirts provoked another round of picture taking, then we were led into the gym.

Inside, a large crowd of people, hot dogs and sodas in hand, were just settling into their seats. Cameramen and reporters trailed us inside, where Erin and I took our places beside Terry

Meeuwsen on some courtside seats. As we did so, the public address system crackled to life. "Ladies and gentlemen, thank you for coming to the Easter Seals All Star Charity Tournament. Tonight we have as our special guests Miss America 1973, Terry Meeuwsen, and two Easter Seals Children, Jean Driscoll and Erin Connolly, along with several distinguished members of the Milwaukee branch of the Easter Seals Committee. Let's give them a warm welcome."

_____

As the crowd roared, I felt myself flush with pride.

_____

As the crowd roared, I felt myself flush with pride. I wished Francie and the boys were there to see all the attention I was getting.

However, once the games began, I soon forgot I was at the event as a poster child. One of the basketball players threw Erin and me each a basketball, and I was much more interested in bouncing this on the side of the court than I was in watching the game.

I was glad my mother had dropped me off instead of coming in. She probably would have forbidden me to run around as I was doing. In the past year I had broken two more bones—first my right leg, then my left ankle—and she was forever telling me to be careful not to slip or fall.

When the final whistle blew, one of the basketball players came over to me. "Do you want to shoot a basket?" he asked.

I nodded. The next thing I knew, two powerful arms were lifting me up and carrying me onto the court.

"Here you go, big girl," player Number Sixty-two said, handing me the ball. I pulled up the sleeves of my sweatshirt and grasped the ball with both hands. As I did so, the player lifted me high into the air. I laughed with exhilaration and threw the ball. It ricocheted off the rim. Camera shutters clicked around me, and I waved at the crowd.

The rest of my year as an Easter Seals poster child was just as much fun. Erin and I attended a number of important breakfasts, lunches, and dinners where we cut ribbons and awarded prizes. We were also guests on *Dialing for Dollars,* a local television show to which viewers at home could call in and win money. At each appearance or event, I became a little more used to my newfound celebrity. Unfortunately, I couldn't resist the urge to brag when I returned home with new clothes and other gifts, and the gap between my siblings and me seemed to widen at about the same rate that my scrapbook filled up with photographs and newspaper clippings about my adventures.

When my time as an Easter Seals poster girl finally ended in May, it was hard to go back to being just plain old Jean Driscoll with the dragging legs. This was not an easy transition, and over the summer I became locked in a constant battle with my mother over what I could and could not do. When I went outside to play in the driveway, she made me wear black rubber over-the-shoe boots to protect the soles of my everyday shoes. I loathed the boots. Everyone else got to wear cool tennis shoes while I was forced to run around in footwear that made me look like a runaway from the fire department. When I complained to my mother that I was getting teased for looking "dorky," she wasn't swayed. She knew how quickly the soles of my shoes wore out and how gloomy and frustrated I was when I had to stay inside for the three days it took to have them resoled. Meanwhile all the other neighborhood kids were outside enjoying themselves.

I knew she was right, but that didn't make the teasing any easier to bear. So, whenever I thought I could get away with it, I would play on the driveway, throwing a basketball or playing tag with the neighboring kids without my rubber overboots.

On the days Mom caught me doing this, I was sent to my room as punishment for my disobedience. There I would spend hours admiring the collection of basketball and volleyball trophies lined up on the dresser my sister and I shared. Of course, they all belonged to Francie, and she hated for me to touch them, so I only picked them up when she wasn't around. I would hold them and imagine I was the one dressed in the MPH Warriors' blue-and-white uniform, throwing the winning basket at the school game or spiking the volleyball over the net to a spot where no one could get it. Then I would imagine myself at an awards banquet, dressed in my yellow lacy dress and receiving the trophy. If I heard someone coming up the stairs, I quickly put the trophy back on the dresser and pretended to be reading. I had no doubt my siblings would tease me if they ever discovered my dream of being an athlete.

As the summer wore on, we all got a little bored, and the twins began talking about an adventure they were planning. Ray and Ron began to nag Mom to let them ride their bikes all the way to our Aunt Joan and Uncle Frankie's house. This was thirteen miles west of us in the small town of Sussex. I seized the opportunity to join in the nagging, pointing out that I was older than the boys and that I should be allowed to ride that far with them. The twins finally wore Mom down, and she agreed to let them go on one condition: that they take me along. Ray and Ron were not at all pleased about this, but Mom stood firm, and I glowed with the thought of riding all the way to Sussex. It seemed such a grown-up thing to do.

I had no doubt my siblings would tease me if they ever discovered my dream of being an athlete.

The following morning we set out. Each of us had wrapped our pajamas and a change of clothes in a brown grocery sack and put them on the carrier on Ron's bike. Ray had a bottle of water, and I had a dime in my pocket to call home in case anything went wrong.

We rode silently down Silver Spring Drive, a busy four-lane street that led out of town. Eventually it became a two-lane highway with a speed limit of fifty-five miles per hour. The traffic was heavy, so the three of us rode our bikes in the gravel on the side of the road. This was fine until we got to a hill. I watched as the twins took the lead. They stood up on their pedals and used the full force of their weight to power their bikes up the incline. I, on the other hand, had to stay seated on my bike because I didn't have the leg strength or the balance to stand on the pedals of my bike and power it forward. Time after time my speed was so slow that the bike wobbled beneath me until I fell onto the gravel. Each time this happened, I picked myself up and tried again. And each time the twins looked back, I was a little farther behind them.

As I struggled up the hill, I wished I had a ten-speed bike like my friend Dawn. I was sure that it would be easier for me to keep my balance if I could keep pedaling faster up the hills. But as much as I wished it, I knew I wasn't likely to convince my parents that a ten-speed bike belonged on the list of items necessary for the family. It had been a big enough event when they bought my present bike at a police auction for ten dollars.

"Keep pedaling!" chided Ron.

"Yeah. You have to pedal a bike to make it go!" Ray added.

Both boys then burst into laughter at Ray's joke, and I felt my face redden with anger and frustration.

"I'm trying!" I yelled up at them, "I can't help it if my legs won't push the pedals."

Finally, half walking, half biking, I made it to the top of the hill where the twins were waiting for me. We didn't stay together for long. They pedaled fast, even down the hills, and soon I watched them disappear around a curve.

"Wait for me!" I yelled, wishing, as I had done a thousand times before, that the twins had my problem and knew what it was like to be constantly trying to catch up.

The next hill was not as steep, and I was over halfway up before I took my first spill. As I brushed myself off and got back on the bike, I knew I couldn't give up, not when I had a goal to work toward. I could see myself biking triumphantly up Aunt Joan's driveway with thirteen miles of cycling under my belt.

All in all, it took us two and a half hours to get to Sussex. We were just at the top of the last hill and five blocks away from Aunt Joan's house when her black Buick pulled up beside us. "I was just coming to look for you!" she yelled as she rolled down the window. "Guess who I've got here?"

I peered into the car and saw my nine-year-old cousin, Polly, who was visiting from northern Wisconsin.

Aunt Joan pulled to the side of the road and got out of the car. "Jean!" she exclaimed. "You must be exhausted. Did you ride all the way?"

"Yes," I said proudly, "I'm doing fine."

Aunt Joan shook her head. "You look flushed to me." She took my arm and started directing me toward the car. "I think you'd better get in the car and let Polly ride your bike the rest of the way."

I felt my mouth drop open in shock. I was only five blocks from the "finish line."

I tried to look casual. "Oh, Aunt Joan, I'll be fine. It's downhill all the way from here. I can manage. Honest I can," I said.

"Come on. Get in the car," she commanded, gesturing for Polly to take my bike.

"But…," I said, desperation edging into my voice.

"No buts, Jean. You've done enough for one day. Now be sensible and get in the car."

The jubilation of being so near to my goal drained from me as I climbed into the front seat of the Buick. Aunt Joan shut the car door after me. She had no idea how crushed I felt. I couldn't believe what was happening.

Aunt Joan waited while the twins and Polly took off for the last half-mile of the journey. Polly turned and smiled at me, but I couldn't smile back. I had been so close to reaching my goal, and it had been ripped away from me.

We spent the night at Aunt Joan's house. Although I started off angry and frustrated, I soon relaxed and began having fun. We played pool and baked cookies that we decorated with M&M's to enjoy with the ice-cream sundaes that Uncle Frankie treated us to after dinner.

I had been so close to reaching my goal.

The following day I was stiff and sore from my tumbles off the bike, but I didn't say a word about it. I had overheard Aunt Joan tell Uncle Frankie that she was going to drive me back to our house, and I was determined not to let that happen. While I may have lost the battle of being allowed to ride the last half-mile of the journey on the way there, I wasn't about to let anything keep me from riding back home with my brothers. Riding there and back had been the whole goal of the trip. I pleaded with Aunt Joan until finally she gave in and packed me a snack so I could ride along with Ray and Ron.

I was pleased to make the entire trip back unaided, but I couldn't shake the feeling of being cheated out of attaining my goal, all because of my "bad" legs. When we finally arrived home, Ray and Ron bragged to their friends about how they were the only two who had completed the entire trip. Every time I heard them say this I fumed inside. I began to fixate on the mobility I would get from a ten-speed bike with gears for all riding conditions. If only there were some way of getting one.

To my surprise, the opportunity to win a ten-speed bike presented itself in my last year at Mother of Perpetual Help School during homeroom. One day the principal announced that there was to be a citywide read-a-thon sponsored by the Multiple Sclerosis Society, and the grand prize was a gift certificate for a brand-new ten-speed bike.

I was giddy with excitement. All I needed to do was get people to pay me to read as many books as it took, and I would have my very own ten-speed! It sounded so simple, and all through science and English I mapped out the neighborhoods I was going to visit on my quest.

As soon as I got home that afternoon, I had a snack and headed out to ride around the neighborhoods.

Once I got to the street I had decided upon, I knocked on every door. I knew most of the people who answered, at least by sight. "How many books do you think you can read?" they would ask.

"Oh, about ten or twelve," I would reply innocently, with every intention of reading thirty or more books.

Soon the five or ten cents a book people sponsored me for began to add up. By the end of the first week I had signed up twenty-three sponsors. Of course, while I had lots of sponsors, I hadn't yet read a single book. That weekend Mom drove me to the local library, where I checked out my limit of books and began reading. Francie looked shocked. "What are you doing with all those books?" she asked.

"I'm going to read them all," I replied proudly.

My sister laughed, "Remember how long it took you to read *Island of the Blue Dolphins* for English class?"

"Well, I'm going to!" I said, although I had to admit she had a point.

Ironically, while I was the one who had to sit out of many activities, Francie was the born reader. Fortunately for me, though, she was now a freshman at Divine Savior Holy Angels High School and was a year too old to qualify for the read-a-thon. Otherwise she may have been my main competition.

Slowly the list of books I had read, or at least skimmed through, grew. And as I compared myself with the other students at school I discovered I was way out in front of them in terms of the money I was raising, though I had no idea how well kids at the other schools in the area were faring.

After a month, I collected all the money from my sponsors and handed it to my homeroom teacher, Mr. Mentch. There was nothing left to do but wait to see who had won the read-a-thon.

Finally, one morning in early March, when I had almost forgotten about the competition, the voice of our principal, Mrs. Miles, crackled over the loud speaker system. "Boys and girls," she began, "I am so proud of every one of the students at Mother of Perpetual Help School who together raised over eight hundred dollars for the Multiple Sclerosis Society through the read-a-thon. You all worked so hard, and I know you will be thrilled to learn we have a winner in our midst."

I took a deep breath and waited, willing Mrs. Miles to say my name.

"Eighth-grader Jean Driscoll has won the grand prize: the gift certificate for a brand-new ten-speed bicycle."

Twenty heads swiveled around to stare at me. I felt myself grinning from ear to ear and going bright red. I could hardly take it in. I had done it! I had won the ten-speed! For the rest of the day, I couldn't concentrate on my schoolwork. I was too busy thinking about what my new bike would look like.

Later that week my parents took me to the local Toys 'R Us store to redeem my gift certificate. I walked down the rows of bikes, taking mental note of the pros and cons of each one. It came down to a choice between a tan Huffy Santa Fe and a silver-and-black Kent. I walked back and forth between them for nearly half an hour, agonizing over which one I liked better.

"You need to make a decision, Jean," I heard Mom say finally. "I need to get Jacques to bed."

"I'm almost done." I took one last look over my shoulder at the silver Kent. It had hard plastic handgrips, while the Huffy had brown spongy ones with hundreds of tiny holes in them. "I'll take the Huffy," I said, allowing the extra comfort of the spongy handgrips and the bike's sportier look to sway me.

"Okay," replied Dad. "Let's go get it."

Mom called a salesperson over and pointed out the bike I had decided to get. He went into the back of the store and came out with a large cardboard box in a cart. I proudly wheeled the cart to the cash register and presented my gift certificate to the cashier.

When we got home, Dad started putting the bike together. I stayed beside him, chattering away as he read the complex instructions on how to assemble the gears and the brakes.

By the time he was finished assembling the Huffy it was bed-
time, and I had to wait until the following morning before I could
ride it.

I awoke several times during the night, thinking about how
lucky I was to have a ten-speed waiting for me downstairs. However, I knew I wouldn't be able to ride my new bike on the street
until the end of April, when the neighborhood police came to
school and set up a licensing station. This was an annual event at
which riders had to maneuver their bikes through a simple obstacle course. A policeman watched for good hand signals and brak-
ing skills. If he observed them, the county licensed both the rider
and the bike to be on the public roads. This licensing event was
three weeks away, and I wondered how I was going to confine
myself to riding in the driveway until then.

As it happened, I couldn't contain myself. One day when my
mother was napping, I sneaked my new bike out the front door of
the house and into the street. I tested the dual handbrakes and pedaled backward, enjoying the rhythmic clicking the sprocket made
as the bike coasted along the street. In no time at all, I was at the
baseball diamond where Ray and Ron were practicing with their
Cub Scout pack. I sat on the bike, holding the fence with my right
hand, and watched them finish up. Then a group of scouts came
running over to me. "Wow! Is this what you won?" asked one of
them.

"Look how cool it is," said another boy admiringly.

"I thought you weren't supposed to have your bike out yet,"
Ron said.

"Yeah," agreed Ray, "I bet Mom doesn't know you're here."

"Come on, guys," I said, trying to think of how to avert disaster. "I'll let you ride it if you don't tell."

"Okay," Ray said. "Hop off and let me ride to the corner and back."

I watched nervously as the twins each took a turn at riding my bike. Then I rode it home, with them running alongside me. I breathed a sigh of relief when I saw that the door to my parents' room was still shut; this meant my mother had not yet awakened. The twins helped me carry the bike noiselessly back into the living room, and I congratulated myself on the successful completion of my clandestine ride.

However, I had overlooked one important detail: There was mud on the tires. My father confronted me with this observation when he sat down to watch the news, and I had to admit I had sneaked the bike out on the road. He forbade me from so much as even sitting on the bike until it had been registered and grounded me until the end of the week. Still, I told myself, the ride had been worth it. I relived it many times in my mind as I waited impatiently for the police licensing station to open. I was sure that once I had permission to ride on the open road I would be unstoppable. That bike was my ticket to freedom that spring of my thirteenth year.

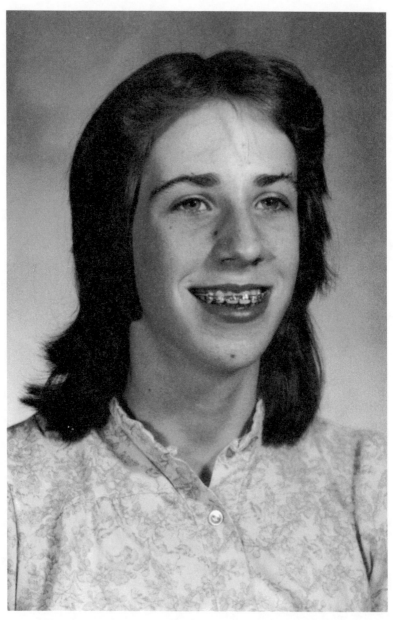

My school photo from freshman year, just before the accident.

FOUR

The Debacle

It was 4:30 in the afternoon on Wednesday, November 12, 1980, less than a week before my fourteenth birthday. I had just finished an after-school baby-sitting job and was riding my ten-speed down the driveway that led from the house to the road. My mind was on the homework I had to do that night. I was now in ninth grade at Divine Savior Holy Angels High School, and even though it was a lot more work than grade school, I loved it. Since I couldn't participate competitively in any sport at school, I made academics my playing field. Doing well in class gave me a sense of identity and accomplishment amid the popularity contests of cheerleading and sports.

I was thinking about the math assignment due at the end of the week as I turned out of the driveway and left onto Fifty-fifth Street. In an instant, I realized that I had turned more sharply than I intended to. At the worst possible moment, my left pedal reached the bottom of its arc. I heard it scrape against the sidewalk, and my bike fell sideways. I clung to it as it went down. Wham! As I slammed onto the pavement, my left hip took the brunt of the impact. I lay there in too much pain to move, listening to the bike wheel spinning on top of me. Though I had no way of knowing it at that moment, I had just experienced one of the defining moments of my life.

I must have stayed there for two or three minutes, immobilized by pain as I had never experienced it before. It shot up and down my left side as if I was being stabbed repeatedly. The minutes passed and the pain slowly subsided enough for me to be able to think straight. I lifted my head and looked around for signs of blood. There were none.

Cautiously, I sat up and glanced around to see if anyone in the house had seen what had happened. I hoped not. This wasn't the first time I had crashed a bike. After one spill I'd even suffered a concussion and a brief bout of amnesia. I didn't want anyone to come running to my aid or, worse still, to call my mother.

**I was shaken up, but I was able to get
back on my bike and ride home.**

Finally the pain subsided enough for me to push the bike off me. Slowly I stood. I was shaken up, but the pain was nowhere as intense as it had been, and I was able to get back on the bike and ride home. All the way, I chided myself for being so stupid. How could I have managed to fall off and hurt myself when I'd been going so slowly? I wasn't even on the street, just someone's driveway! I decided not to tell anyone what had happened.

By the time the dinner dishes were done, I had almost forgotten about the accident. I went down to the basement to watch a favorite television show before starting on my math homework. When I got down there, Ray and Ron already had the station tuned in to the show. The first block of advertisements had just come on when the phone rang upstairs. I heard my father open the door and yell down, "Jean, you have a phone call."

I got up off the couch and took a few steps toward the stairs. I was about halfway across the room when I suddenly felt shooting pains in my left hip. My legs buckled and I fell to the cold concrete floor. I lay there confused. The pain in my hip felt exactly the same as when I fell off my bike. But I hadn't fallen this time; I had just been walking across the room.

"What's wrong?" asked Ray.

"Nothing, I just slipped," I mumbled.

This time the pain subsided more quickly, allowing me to get moving again. I scooted up the stairs on my bottom, then across the kitchen floor to where the phone was dangling by its cord.

The call was from my friend Sally. She had a homework question that we discussed briefly. When the conversation was over, I tried to stand to hang up the phone. However, I discovered I couldn't put any weight on my legs.

My father walked into the room just as I was struggling to stand. "What's wrong, Jean?" he asked.

"I can't stand up," I said. "Something's happened to my leg."

He walked over to me and felt for broken bones. "Well, you haven't broken anything this time, but your hip doesn't look right. I'll go and get your crutches," he said. My dad was trained as a paramedic, though an injured back prevented him from working in that field. He often read my mom's nursing books as well. Since I didn't want to go to the ER, he allowed me to wait and see how it was the next morning.

The next morning I was not in pain, but I still couldn't put any weight on my leg. After breakfast my mother examined me. She looked worried. "Tell me what happened."

As much as I dreaded it, I had to tell my mother about the bike accident: how I had felt okay enough to ride the bike home afterward and how the pain had returned that night. I did make one adjustment to my story, though. I couldn't bear for anyone to know that I'd only been going down a driveway, so I told her I was riding fast down Custer Street and turning onto Fifty-fifth when my pedal hit the pavement.

Mom sighed wearily. "I'll call the doctor," she said.

My heart sank. My mother told me that Dr. Flatley was the best orthopedic doctor in town, but I dreaded the way he manipulated my body without any apparent concern for the pain. When Mom got off the phone, she told me the doctor was out of town at a conference and wouldn't be back until the weekend. "Do you think you can walk on your crutches until then?" she asked.

I nodded, knowing that Mom would be very reluctant to take me to a doctor who didn't know my case history.

For the next two days I hobbled to school on my crutches. Sometimes I felt normal, but at other times the searing pain took my breath away.

On Saturday morning, instead of going to bed after working her usual third shift, my mother drove me to the medical center. We listened to the radio on the way, and I tried to concentrate on the songs and not on whatever might be ahead for me. Still, worrisome thoughts managed to creep in. Would I miss any school next week? What was the doctor going to do with me? How long would I have to use crutches?

At the medical center, an attendant brought me a hospital wheelchair and I went off for x-rays. When I got back to the emergency room, the doctor was waiting for me. He had a grim look on his face and my x-rays in his hand. I watched intently as he stared over the top of his bifocal glasses at my mother.

"Jean is going to need a series of hip surgeries, the first one being a triple osteotomy in order to position the angle of her hip correctly. Before that she'll need traction to realign her hip joint. Following each operation she'll need a spica cast. At some stage during the year she's going to have to undergo a muscle transfer. I'm not sure when; it will depend on the rate of healing and the depth we can get in the socket."

Dr. Flatley paused for a moment, and Mom asked a question.

While I couldn't understand much of what the doctor said, the words "triple osteotomy" stuck in my mind. I tried to follow the conversation as the doctor held up one or another of my x-rays and pointed things out to my mother. After about ten minutes of going back and forth, I heard the doctor use a phrase I did understand: "body cast."

Body cast? My head began to spin. Was Dr. Flatley referring to a cast that covered my entire body from my toes on up? I felt the color drain from my face as he looked at me. He folded his arms and said wryly, "This is quite a debacle, Jean, isn't it?"

I had no idea what *debacle* meant, but the way the doctor said it, I knew it must be something serious and awful.

My mother and the doctor spoke for a few more minutes,

arranging for me to be admitted to the hospital after church the following day. I understood that I was to go into surgery Monday morning.

On the way home from the hospital, I asked my mother what was going to happen to me, but even she seemed unsure. She looked worried and distracted by our hospital visit. I, on the other hand, couldn't imagine any hospital procedure that could keep me inactive for more than a few weeks, even if it did involve a body cast.

How wrong I was.

_____

I was to go into surgery Monday morning.

_____

As arranged, Mom brought me back to the hospital after church on Sunday and I was admitted as a patient. Since parents didn't stay in the hospital with their kids back then, there wasn't much to do that evening except watch television. Nurses came in to check my vitals, and I wanted desperately to ask them questions about what was going to happen to me. But I was too shy. I knew that the surgery was going to prepare me to go into traction, but I had little sense of what that would involve. All that I knew about traction came from slapstick movies on TV. I awoke several times during the night, my heart thumping, panicked at the thought of what might be going to happen to me. But of all of the images I conjured up, nothing came close to the shocking reality that I faced on Monday morning.

At nine o'clock sharp, I was wheeled into the operating room. I lay fully awake as the staff arrived. Wide-eyed, I watched as the attending physician picked up a huge needle from a stainless steel tray and cleaned a spot on the outside of my leg. I clenched my fists so tightly I could feel my fingernails stabbing into my palms. Without even looking at me, the physician jabbed me with the very large needle. I started to sob as I watched blood spurt out of my leg. Oblivious to my pain, he reached for another, equally long, needle and lifted it into position. Indignation rose in me. I knew that some kids with spina bifida didn't have any feeling in their legs, but I thought he should have known how much feeling I had.

I sobbed bitterly through three more needles and then watched in horror as he picked up a drill. Terror gripped me as I realized he was going to use it on my thigh. I began flailing my arms and yelling at the doctor, trying to get him to stop. Then I began screaming with all my might. One of the nurses pinned my arms down, while another held a blanket over my head.

Terror engulfed me and I screamed on.

I felt the pressure of the drill biting into my flesh, churning through my skin. The nauseating smell of burning flesh and the whine of the drill filled the room. The drill became more high-pitched as it hit my bone. The pressure increased as the doctor bore down harder on my leg. Vibrations jarred my whole body. I was living my worst nightmare.

Finally everything stopped and the nurse pulled the blanket off my head. I looked down to see what had been done to me. Like a giant pincer, a stainless steel triangle stuck out of both sides of my thigh. Around the pin was a thin circle of clotted blood on the bandages.

I was wheeled from surgery into an unfamiliar room with a traction bed set up in it. Once I had been lifted onto the bed, a nurse looped a rope through the metal triangle. I watched as she fed the rope through a pulley and down over the end of my bed. As she worked, the nurse explained there were weights on the foot of the bed. The idea was to put pressure on my hip in order to pull it back into line with my hip socket.

My mother came to see me that night. The following day, Tuesday, November 18, my entire family arrived to help me celebrate my fourteenth birthday. My brothers and sister were alternately fascinated to see me in traction and repulsed by the pin sticking out from both sides of my leg. The slightest movement near the bed would make the weight swing, causing pain to shoot through my body. I couldn't enjoy my cherry chip cake; I was too busy begging my siblings not to go near the end of the bed.

The following Saturday was the date of my long-anticipated fourteenth birthday party. Instead of my friends coming to my house for cake and games as I had planned, Mom arranged for nine of my girlfriends to meet me in the waiting room of the fifth floor. The nurses rolled my traction bed out there, and I had a makeshift party. Once again, I spent most of my energy fending off any movement near my bed, as I couldn't tolerate the pain.

This period of being in traction lasted ten days before my hip was pronounced ready for surgery. I was transferred by ambulance from Good Samaritan Medical Center to Milwaukee Children's Hospital, about five blocks away.

Before I went to sleep on the night before my first scheduled surgery, a nurse came into my room with a large piece of paper. She taped it to the head of my bed. On the paper were written the letters "NPO."

"What does that mean?" I asked.

"Oh," she replied, "you should have one last drink now because you won't be allowed anything else to eat or drink until after the operation tomorrow."

Early the next morning I was scrubbed with a strong-smelling soap, called Betadine, that left my skin feeling sticky. The nurse told me I would be wheeled off soon. I waited, trying desperately not to relive my last experience in an operating room. I watched as my fellow patients were served a morning drink…then lunch. By now I was feeling very hungry. Finally, at three o'clock, an attendant came to wheel me away.

In contrast to my traction experience, I was given an anesthetic immediately, and I drifted off to sleep before I could count to ten. I woke up four hours later in the recovery room. My whole lower body felt as though it was on fire. The tiniest movement sent waves of pain pulsating through me. I lay perfectly still for a long time before I gathered the courage to lift my left arm very slowly. I turned my arm toward my body until I came to the cast. I ran my hand slowly up and down it about six inches then lay my arm back, exhausted.

I groaned and a nurse looked up. "Would you like something for the pain?" she asked.

"Yes," I replied, my fear of needles taking second place to my need for relief.

As she swabbed my arm, the nurse apologized. "I'm going to give you a shot of Demerol, and I'm afraid it's going to burn as it goes in. We normally put it into the leg, but with the cast on, everything's going to have to go into your arm."

The nurse was right. The Demerol burned almost as much as my hip, but within minutes I was feeling drowsy again. Soon after that, nausea set in and I accepted the offer of a second shot to stop me from throwing up.

On the second day, as the shot wore off, I decided to try to look down at my cast. With the utmost care I lifted my head from the pillow. The first thing I saw was a patch of blood on my cast about the size of a baseball. I lay back down quickly as the reality of major surgery rolled across me in waves of panic. I had just been through one surgery, but hadn't the doctor told my mother I had at least two more to go?

I tried to imagine what it would be like to be in this cast for six months.

It was hours before I was able to look again. This time I knew to expect the blood, and I could see that the body cast went from just below my chest, completely down my left leg to my foot, and partly down my right leg to just above the knee. There was a two-foot bar plastered in place from above my right knee to the base of my left shin to keep my legs set at a prescribed angle. I tried to imagine what it would be like to be in this cast for six months or even a year, but I couldn't.

All in all, I lay in bed for four days, drifting in and out of consciousness, until the doctor announced that it was time for me to be weaned off my pain-killing shots and to begin to move around. Instead of the Demerol shots, I was given Tylenol with codeine, which took about forty-five minutes to work. The nurse told me this was standard procedure, but I resented the time it took the Tylenol to work, especially since the pain was intense.

In accordance with the doctor's orders, two nurses lifted me off my bed and onto a narrow stainless-steel cart with rails on the sides. They pushed me out of my room and into the hallway. I was able to lie on my stomach and look ahead of me and to both sides. One of the nurses wheeled me to the playroom, where other young patients were playing games and doing puzzles and crafts. The first time I visited the playroom I was in too much pain to watch the other children, but after several days I began to join in a little. I played cards and other board games. I hated to be alone and sometimes in the evening, when the playroom was closed, the nurses would wheel me out to the nurses' station and park me there. That way I could chat with them and watch what was happening on the floor.

My mother used to visit me each morning after work (she was on night shift then), and I looked forward to her coming. Whenever she had the time she would gently give me a sponge bath. It felt so good!

It was nearly four weeks from the day of my admission to the time I was discharged. I had missed Thanksgiving, and I was eager to be home for Christmas.

I couldn't fit into Mom's car so I was loaded into an ambulance. As I was wheeled on the gurney, the cold December air whipped around my head and shoulders. It was the first time I had felt the wind in a month. Winter had set in while I was in the hospital.

When we got to my house, the paramedics had to tilt the stretcher sideways to get me through the narrow front door. I was taken into the living room and transferred to a hospital bed that had been set up there for me. The first thing I noticed was that the piano was gone. When I asked Mom what had happened to it, she told me it had been sold to make enough room for my bed. My bed replacing the piano seemed to epitomize everything I felt at that moment. All my life I had struggled to be independent like my sister and brothers, and now here I was displacing the piano everyone loved so much. I wanted to tell everyone that as much as they wished I didn't have to lie in the middle of the living room, I wished it a hundred times more.

My siblings in 1985: behind me from left to right are
Frances, Ron, and Jacques; Ray is with me on the stool.

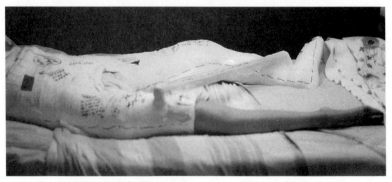

My "plaster garment" ran from toe to rib cage.

FIVE

LIFE SENTENCE

After the paramedics left the house, my mother brought me a glass of milk and a sandwich, told me she was going to bed (this was her "nighttime"), and left me alone to stare at my surroundings. I could see through two windows from where I lay. One framed the bushes on the right side of our driveway and part of the roof of our neighbor's house. Through the other, I could see a bare branch of our elm tree and about six feet of another neighbor's sloping driveway.

As I lay there, the reality of what I was facing began to sink in. I had felt sorry for myself while I was in hospital, but I could see that being at home was going to be a lot more lonely. The hospital was a bustling place. There was always a nurse coming or going, not to mention the opportunity to be wheeled out into a public area where I could play with the other kids or eavesdrop at the nurses' station. At home, everything was silent while my brothers and sister were at school. Mom couldn't sleep with the TV or radio on. During the day, there would be no one to talk to, no entertainment, and no one to joke with. The dreariness of what lay ahead engulfed me, and silent tears trickled off my face and onto the pillow.

Things got a little better after my siblings arrived home, though. Ray made me a snack, and Ron sat on the couch and told me about his latest basketball practice. When Francie came home, she complained about how stuck up all the girls were in her class and then flopped down in front of the TV to watch *Gilligan's Island.* I was thrilled to have the distraction, though I urged her to turn it down so it wouldn't awaken Mom.

Jacques, in an attempt to be kind, volunteered to run up to my room and gather up a notebook, pencils and pens, brush, comb, and a hand mirror. I laid them out neatly on the card table beside my bed.

As the days wore on, I became desperate for a way to connect with the outside world. My father came to my rescue, devising a way to extend the telephone so that it was within my reach. The only phone in the house was hung on the wall in the kitchen. Dad made a wooden cradle so I could hang the handset on the wall beside my bed instead. Then he stretched the phone cord around the wall from the kitchen to the living room. As long as my family members remembered to hang the phone up in the wooden cradle instead of on the wall in the kitchen, I had access to it.

The telephone became a lifesaver for me. I regularly called several of the nurses I had made friends with at the hospital. I was mindful, though, that I could become a pest and they might stop talking to me. To avoid this, I followed a strict protocol. I knew the shift roster for each of the six nurses I called, and I didn't call them within an hour of starting or finishing work. I allowed myself only one call a week. Angie was the exception to my rule. If I had a brief conversation with her one day, then I felt I could call her again in two days. But if we had chatted for more than ten minutes, I waited three days before I called again.

I would talk with each nurse about what was going on at the hospital with the patients I knew, about their romantic interests, their pets, and their dinner plans. I thought about where each of them would be during different times of the day, living vicariously through their experiences.

At home, the novelty of having a sister in a body cast wore off quickly. Getting things for someone who couldn't do anything for herself lost its appeal, and I found myself at the mercy of whomever I could beg to bring me a snack or turn on the TV. Time moved so slowly for me that I noticed every minute pass. I spent the long, lonely hours during the day playing pointless games I invented. One involved trying not to look at the digital clock on the opposite wall until it displayed a time that made some kind of pattern. For example, I gave myself a point if I "caught" the clock reading 12:34, 1:11, 1:23, 2:22, 2:34, or 3:33, and two points if I looked when it said 11:18. That was my birthday.

Two weeks after arriving back home, I was glad to learn that Mom had arranged for the Milwaukee Public School System to provide a tutor for me. I had spent many hours worrying about how I was going to keep up with my friends. I didn't want my grades to slip in what I still believed would be the short period of time before I went back to school. However, working with my tutor was not an ideal arrangement. She only visited for two hours a week, between eleven o'clock and noon on Tuesdays and Thursdays. During the rest of the time, I was assigned chapters to read and questions to answer from my English and U.S. history textbooks.

Without the other students from my class to compete against and interact with, schoolwork quickly became boring. Before long I found myself totally unmotivated, doing the least amount of work I could possibly get away with. Science classes were particularly dull since I had to read about the experiments instead of doing them. I plodded on, but for the first time in my life, schoolwork became pure drudgery.

One of the highlights of my week was getting my hair washed.

The pathetic part was that I really had nothing better to do than study. Indeed, one of the highlights of my week was getting my hair washed. This was a long procedure, and Mom had to make time in her overcrowded schedule to do it. She would get one of the twins to drag a metal trash can in from outside and then line it with a plastic garbage bag. I would flip myself onto my stomach and pull myself forward until my head was hanging over the edge of the bed. Meanwhile, Mom filled a pitcher with water. When everything was ready, she placed a towel around my neck and poured the water over my head. It would cascade down into the garbage can. She would then shampoo my hair and rinse out the soap with several more pitchers of water. Finally, I would towel my hair dry and comb it while one of the twins was conscripted to help Mom carry the water-filled trash can outside and dump it in the backyard.

If this was the high point of my week, the low points were when my mother attended to my bathroom needs. Mom was so overworked that we had to do things on her schedule, not ours. I was no exception. She took care of my needs not only with the efficiency of a well-trained nurse, but often with the same detachment. When she was in "nurse mode," sometimes she didn't seem to take into account that I was in the living room or that other people might also be in there. Sometimes hot tears of indignation streamed down my cheeks when I was stuck on the bedpan in the middle of the living room with my brothers and their friends in the same room, but my mother was too exhausted to pander to a teenager's sense of modesty. How I longed for the blue privacy curtains that had enveloped me in the hospital! Yet I realized Mom was doing the best she could. She did all the bathroom duties as it was too embarrassing for me to have my dad help.

As the days dragged on, I found myself fantasizing about my next visit to the hospital. At particularly lonely moments I even thought of ways to get back there sooner. I imagined flinging myself out of the bed and onto the floor. I felt sure this would warrant at least an overnight stay. But as appealing as the thought of going back to the hospital was, I couldn't bring myself to carry out the plan. I was too scared of dislocating my hip again and suffering through another round of traction.

But actually I didn't have long to wait for the next visit. I was readmitted to the hospital in January for an operation to deepen my hip socket. A third operation in March worked again on the angle of my hip. In August, Dr. Flatley performed two final operations, the first one to take muscle from the top of my thigh and attach it around my hip to give the joint more strength. Ten days later, just as I was beginning to recover from that procedure, he performed an operation on my right hip to prevent it from dislocating in the same way that the left one had. Following that surgery, the body cast was extended all the way down both legs.

Finally, after the longest eleven months of my life, the day arrived to have the body cast removed. I should have been excited, but I was terrified. This was the first time since the traction pin had been installed in my leg that I was not going to be put under an anesthetic while something major was done to me. When I spotted the circular saw on the counter I panicked. My eyes got big and began to flood with tears.

After the longest eleven months of my life, the day arrived to have the body cast removed.

"It's going to be okay, Jean," said Noreen, one of the nurses.

"But how deep are you going to cut me?"

Noreen smiled and picked up the saw. "It's going to be okay," she repeated. "Look, this doesn't really cut. It vibrates." She held the blade on her hand. "Even if it touches your skin it won't cut it."

"Oh," I said, knowing that my fears should have been alleviated but feeling more tense than ever.

"Are you ready?" asked the doctor.

I didn't say a word.

"Aha! I see I have instructions!" he chuckled, tracing his hand down the dotted line that Angie, another nurse, had jokingly drawn down the length of my cast. In one spot she had written, "Cut here" with arrows pointing to the dotted line. I had thought it was funny too, but I couldn't bring myself to laugh right then.

My knuckles turned white as the saw started to whine. Fine powder flew around the room as the blade churned though the plaster. The vibrations racked my body, but as Noreen had promised, the procedure didn't hurt. Once the saw had cut through the plaster in one spot, the doctor picked up a huge instrument that looked something like a pair of scissors with a vice on the end. He inserted this under the plaster and proceeded to crack me open like a giant lobster.

It took about twenty minutes to go all the way around, then two nurses stepped up and lifted the top half of the plaster shell off me. I was still encased in enough cotton to make me look like a mummy. Noreen began cutting this away, and I prepared myself to be lying naked in a room full of people.

It took six nurses to lift me out of the bottom half of the cast. They supported every joint in my body, so that nothing would be left to sag. It was a weird feeling to be lifted onto a sheet after spending so many months in a cast. The pain in my hips and legs was almost unbearable. My limbs had been straight for so long, it was impossible to move them any closer together without agony. But I didn't have the strength to continually hold them apart. The nurses came to my rescue, sliding several pillows between my legs and putting one under each knee and heel.

I was wheeled back to my room on a gurney. When I got there, I braced myself to see what I looked like. Cautiously, I lifted the sheet and looked down. I put my head quickly back on the pillow, grossed out by the glimpse of my own body. My skin hung off me in long shreds and most of it was still a brownish color from the Betadine that had been used to clean the areas where I'd had surgery. Coarse black hair had grown thick on my legs. I'd also seen the various scars I had on my lower body from the surgeries and staples.

I was so shaken I didn't look down again until the following day. That was when Angie came in to announce I was going to have my first bath. I had looked forward to a bath for so long, but not one like this. I felt as wobbly as a bowl of Jell-O as four nurses lowered me into a deep tub of warm water, my body protesting the slightest touch. Angie produced a four-inch-long nylon scrubbing brush.

"I can't stand to see those hairy legs a moment longer!"

"I know this is going to hurt," she said. "But we have to start getting rid of the dead skin. The only way is to soak and scrub. It's going to take several days to do it all."

I lay there in silent agony as Angie began scrubbing my skin. Every nerve in my lower body screamed with pain, but there was no choice. The top layers of dead skin had to come off. I was so glad when it was time to be lifted back into my bed and to have the pillows propped around me again.

Now that this fresh assault on my body had begun, I was eager to get rid of the gorilla-like black hair on my legs. I implored every nurse that came by my room to shave them for me. Later that night, Cindy responded.

"I can't stand to see those hairy legs a moment longer!" she joked as she filled a basin with warm water. Then she took a razor and began shaving them meticulously. When she was finished I couldn't find the right words to thank her. I was so relieved that none of my visitors would have to see my legs the way they had been.

After two weeks, I was discharged from the hospital for the last time. It was a day I had anticipated for so long, a new beginning. Even though I couldn't walk, I knew there were no more operations ahead of me. I also knew that my recovery—and eventual ability to walk better than ever—depended upon my tenacity in the rehabilitation process.

Coaxing the strength and flexibility back into my hips and legs was an excruciatingly painful process, but I was determined to try as hard as I could to get strong again. Our medical insurance didn't allow for regular physical therapy sessions at the house, so I had to devise a way to keep going on my own. I knew I needed to start by getting my knees to bend again. I scooted to the side of the bed, allowing gravity to do its work, slowly forcing my legs toward the floor. I would sit there, bearing the pain as long as I possibly could before scooting back until the mattress supported my legs once again. Then I would roll carefully onto my stomach and prop myself up on my elbows. This movement sent shooting pains up my back, but I knew it was helping my hips to become flexible once again.

I would also time myself to see how long I could sit up. This was even more difficult than getting my knees to bend. Not only was my back very stiff, but the scar tissue from the various operations I had undergone burned as I pulled it in different ways. At first I could only sit up for three minutes, but by the time I was scheduled to go back to the hospital for a checkup a couple of weeks later, I was up to sitting for twenty minutes. I could hardly wait to show my nurse friends the progress I was making.

It was just after two o'clock in the afternoon when Dr. Flatley came into the examination room at the hospital. He had my latest x-rays in his hand and a grim look on his face. I tried to think what it could mean, but I had no clue. As far as I could tell everything was progressing well. I had no inkling that I was about to receive a life sentence.

Dr. Flatley adjusted his bifocals as he looked down at me. "I'm very sorry," he said, looking more distressed than I'd ever seen him. "I've done everything I can for you, Jean, but your hip is showing signs of dislocating again. You simply don't have the muscle density to hold it in place, and it would be useless to attempt any more muscle transplants. You'll have to get used to things the way they are."

I felt my heart beating hard. What was he saying? Doctors were supposed to fix people! He had told me that I was going to be better, that I'd be able to walk again. And now? Had I endured all those months, all that pain for nothing? I was shaken to my core.

I heard Mom sigh deeply, but neither of us spoke. After a long pause, Dr. Flatley addressed my mother. "The best thing she can do is to keep working on her flexibility. Jean needs to get up on her crutches and start putting weight on her legs and hips to strengthen them as much as possible. It's not the outcome we had all hoped for, but I've done everything I can, as you know. I've deepened the hip socket, changed the angle of the joint, transplanted muscle, but it isn't enough. Jean is going to need to use crutches or a wheelchair to get around for the rest of her life. She can use crutches around the house, but for school and longer distances she'll have to be in a wheelchair."

When I heard those words, everything inside of me stopped. I went numb from the inside out. The promise of walking better had sustained me through five rounds of surgery and eleven long, lonely months of recovery. But now, instead of being cured, I was

---

**The independence I had struggled so
hard all my life to achieve had been
yanked away from me.**

---

worse off than before. From now on I was going to need help from crutches, from a wheelchair, from other people. The independence I had struggled so hard all my life to achieve had been yanked away from me. It was incomprehensible, unfathomable. Me, in a wheelchair, handicapped, watching from the sidelines as everyone around me enjoyed their lives.

When I got home, I was still numb. I couldn't bring myself to talk to anyone except to ask for the most basic things. I didn't want to watch television, call my nurse friends, or even eat. My anguish distilled itself into one bitter question: *Why me? Why are you always picking on me, God?*

As if to highlight my fate, Francie, who was only a year older than me, was trying out her own independence. The week after I received my appalling news, Francie got her first job at a Mexican takeout restaurant. She spent her earnings on makeup and new clothes, which she showed me before going out on various dates. I tried to be happy for her but found it impossible. I watched her silently, wondering how God could have been so cruel as to dump all the defects in the family on me. The unfairness of it overwhelmed me. I felt as if I was entering a dark and endless tunnel.

The blue vinyl hospital wheelchair parked in the hallway and the pair of crutches in the corner of the room symbolized everything I hated about my new reality. I swore to myself that I would never use either of them.

When I absolutely had to move around, to use the bathroom or to find a snack, I used the office chair with tiny wheels that had been brought down from my room upstairs. I didn't have the leg strength to propel myself along on it, and my legs weren't long enough anyway, so I moved myself by pushing off with my hands against the walls and furniture.

On November 18, 1981, my fifteenth birthday, I sat silently in bed, continuing to think about the year I'd wasted. This time a year ago I was in the hospital, in traction. I'd had hope then: hope that I would walk again. I'd also had friends. Although Kathleen had continued to call, communication with the other friends I made during my brief time at Divine Savior Holy Angels High School had dwindled to almost nothing. Something had to change.

So, on that birthday, after two weeks of sulking over Dr. Flatley's words, I realized—although I hated to admit it to myself—that it was no fun being angry and rude all the time. I was also extremely bored. There was a world outside our house: a world I couldn't access from my office chair. I stared at the crutches in the corner of the room. *Should I try them out on my birthday?* I asked myself. Finally, I scooted over to them in the office chair.

I grabbed the crutches—one in each hand—and tried to push myself up onto them, but I wasn't strong enough. Instead, I held them both in one hand and worked my way back to the bed. I transferred myself to the edge of the mattress and set the tips of the crutches on the floor. Cautiously, I eased myself down onto them. Once my feet were on the floor I tried to straighten my back, but the scar tissue from my operations kept me bent over. I focused all of my concentration on keeping my balance as I made my way to the bathroom, sticking close to the walls in case I needed to lean on them for extra support.

I could hear my mother in the kitchen talking to a neighbor. I hoped she wouldn't see me, but she did. "That's the first time Jean has used her crutches since she has been home," I heard her say in a surprised voice.

I was embarrassed that she'd seen me. Now my silent protest was over. It was no use hiding in my bed any longer. I knew I had to start moving ahead. I couldn't let the fact that the doctor had not been able to fix my hip joint dominate my future. Somehow I would have to find a way to adjust to a whole new life.

My favorite nurse, Angie (pictured here with her family),
kept me laughing.

SIX

BETRAYED BY MY BODY

"Fourteen months! It's been fourteen months since you were at school last? Wow, time flies."

I looked up at Julie and nodded. "Well, it didn't for me," I said, laughing nervously. "I'm *so* glad to be back."

"We're all glad to see you too," said Julie, fidgeting with the strap on her backpack and looking off down the hallway. "If you need anything, just ask. I have to go now. Bye."

"Bye," I said, watching her brown plaid skirt disappear down the hallway. I'd always been short for my age, but being relegated to a perpetual sitting position had created a new reality for me. I found I had to tilt my neck at a seventy-degree angle to look into someone's face, and then I wasn't looking into the person's eyes but up his or her nose. Being down so low made me feel isolated from normal human interaction in a way I had not anticipated.

"Yeah, if you need anything," Mary echoed, "I'm here to help too."

"Thanks," I mumbled, wishing I had the courage to plead my case: I don't want your *help*. I don't *need* your help. I want to be your friend.

By the time homeroom was over I was glad to move on to classes where the spotlight would be on the subject at hand and not on me. I wheeled down the corridor and onto the elevator that took me to the second floor and my sophomore English class.

Mr. Grandy must have known I was coming because he had a textbook already signed out for me. He smiled and welcomed me back, then asked one of the girls to take the chair away from a desk so I could wheel my chair up to it.

As soon as I was settled he cleared his throat. "We're continuing on page 125," he began. "We've all read the poem 'Thanatopsis,' and I'm sure the first thing you noticed was that it's written in iambic pentameter, unlike *Paradise Lost,* which is written in blank verse. Let's have a look at the first verse of 'Thanatopsis.' Amy, please read it, then comment on the stressed and unstressed syllables in each stanza."

I watched as Amy took a moment and began confidently: "To him who in the love of Nature holds, Communion with her visible forms, she speaks…"

I felt myself shrinking farther back into my wheelchair, stunned by what I was hearing. Whatever had happened to grammar and punctuation? I had never heard of iambic pentameter. Had the class learned some kind of foreign language while I was away?

My heart raced for the rest of the period as I began to wonder how I would ever catch up. Obviously my public-school tutor at home had not been covering all the material my private high-school class had been covering.

I was completely and utterly lost!

Like a recurring nightmare, the scenario repeated itself throughout the morning. In math we were studying geometry with postulates and theorems, and in history the class discussed the reasons why the Articles of Confederation failed. I had no clue about what was being discussed and was relieved when lunchtime finally arrived.

As I entered the cafeteria I expected everyone to be seated where they had been when I left, but then I realized there was now a new group of freshmen, and my friends were sitting in the sophomore area. I wheeled myself over to Kathleen.

"How's it going so far?" she asked.

I could see it was going to be impossible for me to catch up with the rest of the class.

"Oh, it's okay," I said. I was far too embarrassed to tell her the truth. Not understanding the lessons would have been just one more thing that made me different from everyone else. I did concede to having a little difficulty in one area, though. "I didn't understand what the math teacher was talking about," I admitted.

"Oh, don't worry about that!" Kathleen said reassuringly. "He's got a strong accent, and none of us understands what he's saying."

I smiled weakly. I knew she was trying to make me feel better, but the truth was, even if he'd spoken with a perfect Midwestern accent I wouldn't have understood a word of what he said.

Lunch involved a round of casual conversations. Many girls came and told me they were glad to see me back at school. A lot of them seemed uncomfortable to see me in a wheelchair—about as uncomfortable as I felt being in it. The conversations with them were short, and the girls looked relieved as they hurried back to their circle of friends as soon as it was polite to do so.

By the end of the day I was emotionally exhausted. Socially, things had not gone as well as I'd hoped, but I could accept that it would take time for friendships to rekindle; it was the academic aspect of school that had totally shocked me. I was in over my head and I knew it. I could see it was going to be impossible for me to catch up with the rest of the class. I realized I should own up to my parents and start over again as a freshman, but I couldn't bring myself to admit that I had lost a whole year of school because of my stupid accident. As it happened, I didn't have to come clean with my parents. My academic struggles were soon dwarfed by the events that followed my January return to school.

One Saturday morning as I was getting out of the shower, I sat down on the edge of the bathtub to dry my feet. When I got up, I noticed a yellowish discharge on the tub. I knew immediately where it must have come from. A week before I had scraped my bottom on the aluminum track for the glass shower door. It wasn't much of an injury and I hadn't worried about it. After all, I'd had scrapes before on my elbows and knees from when I'd fallen off my bicycle. These had all healed up fine, and so would the scrape on my bottom. However, I had noticed that this scrape was taking awhile to heal. Now, looking at the yellow discharge on the edge of the bathtub, I concluded it might be infected.

I began to worry. What if something was seriously wrong with me? My mother was in bed, so I called for my dad to come and have a look.

He was silent for a long time.

"What does it look like?" I asked.

"This is bad, Jean," he said. "Really, really bad. You've got a wound here, and it's oozing. How did you get it?"

I told him about my scrape, and he insisted on waking up Mom so she could look at it. By ten o'clock that morning I was laying bottom up on an examination table at the Good Samaritan Medical Center.

"Come and look at this, Mrs. Driscoll," Dr. Flatley said. "This pressure sore goes clear down to the bone."

With that he took a cotton swab and stuck it into the wound. He held it out so I could see it. "I can touch your bone with this cotton swab," he said. "You have a bad infection. If it hadn't been found, it could have gone into your bloodstream and killed you." Turning to my mother he said, "I'd like Dr. White to take a look at this. He's a plastic surgeon. I'll be back in a moment."

Dr. Flatley stepped out of the room, and I turned my head to look at my mother. I was too stunned to say anything. I felt totally betrayed by my body, and I hated it even more than I normally did.

"How did it happen?" my mother asked in exasperation.

"All I did was scrape my bottom on the track on the side of the bathtub," I replied, confused that such a small incident could become potentially fatal.

"It's a pressure sore," said my mother, pausing for emphasis. "A pressure sore that has been left to run its course for far too long. You should have told me about it long ago."

"I'm sorry," I said lamely.

The two doctors came back into the room. I'd never seen Dr.

White before, but I remembered several of the nurses gushing over his good looks. I could see why. He was young with a nice tan, beautiful eyes, and a friendly smile. And now he was going to examine my behind! I was not ready for this.

"Mrs. Driscoll, Jean," he said, nodding a greeting to each of us before focusing his attention on my infected bottom. He poked and prodded. I could feel pressure but no pain.

"You're right," he said to Dr. Flatley. "She needs to be admitted immediately. It's a good thing it was caught in time."

Emergency surgery was scheduled for early Monday morning, and by Sunday night I was back in a blue hospital gown, lying flat on my stomach, with the dreaded "NPO" sign hanging over my bed. I had plenty to think about. Dr. Flatley had given me a crash course in pressure sores, saying they could be caused by rubbing or pressure put on one spot of skin for too long, or by not shifting my body weight often enough as I sat in my chair. Of course, this information was all useless to me now. Since I'd never had problems with pressure sores before, even when I was using the chair, no one had told me much about them. Apparently, I had to brace myself for the possibility that I was going to die. *From what?* I asked myself. Was my body so useless that scraping it against a metal track could kill me?

Dr. White operated on me early Monday morning. He cleaned out the wound and cut away the dead flesh. Then he sliced open the back of my leg and cut out healthy tissue, which he transplanted into the hole where the sore was.

When I woke up, I had a scar two feet long from my bottom down the back of my leg. It must have had at least forty staples in it, and for once I was grateful that I didn't have much feeling there. Instead of going back to a normal bed, I found myself in a special bed, called a bead bed. I lay on millions of tiny, sandlike beads of silicon that were covered with a porous plastic material. An electric blower forced the beads to circulate. These buoyed me up, creating a bed of warm air for me. The bed felt wonderful, although I had trouble staying hydrated because of the drying effect of the warm air. The nurses assured me, however, that it would help me to recover more quickly and avoid forming more bedsores as I lay there. The downside was that I couldn't be put on a cart and wheeled out into the corridor to chat with the nurses because the bed was plugged into a wall socket.

One week went by and then another as I waited for the injury to heal so I could get back to school again. I dreaded falling even farther behind. Finally, after staring at the hospital ceiling and walls for two weeks, I was allowed to go home. Dr. White told me I could sit up for ten minutes at a time. The rest of my time was spent lying on my stomach or my side. The doctor also told me that when I finally got back in the wheelchair, I would have to learn to shift my weight around. I had never thought about shifting my weight before. It seemed strange to have to make a conscious effort to do something other people did automatically.

At home I worried about making the tiniest movement. I was scared to death that I would break open the incision on my bottom and not even notice it. I had a mirror so I could see the incision, but

I didn't want to look. It was just too devastating for me to see what a simple scrape could now lead to.

Finally, in late February, Dr. White told me I could return to school. I had been absent for a month. I was embarrassed to go back, though. Last time, everyone knew I'd had a bike accident. This time, I wondered how many students knew I'd had a month off because of a sore on my bottom.

It was just too devastating to see what a simple scrape could now lead to.

At least this time I wasn't shocked to discover I was once again way out of my depth in every subject. I struggled through the rest of the year and my final report card told the story. It was all *D*s and *F*s. There was no question about it. The principal insisted that I repeat tenth grade at Divine Savior Holy Angels High School. By the time summer started, DSHA had become the focal point of all my anger and frustration. I set about convincing my parents they should let me transfer to Custer High School, where I would need only eighteen credits to graduate, not the twenty-six required at DSHA. I was born a year behind Francie, and I was determined to graduate a year behind her as well. Anything else was unacceptable to me.

Summer should have been a time to relax and recover from the stress I'd been through during the past two years, but it turned out to be anything but that. In April I had noticed a small sore forming in the same place as my original pressure sore, but again I hadn't thought much of it. I was certain I hadn't scraped myself or irritated my skin this time, so I was confident it was nothing much. After the last fiasco, though, I decided to show it to my mother just to be sure.

"Oh, Jean!" she exploded. "How could you let this happen?"

"It's not bad this time, is it?" I was on the verge of tears.

"It looks bad to me. Pressure sores don't always show on the skin surface. From the feel of it this is serious." She sighed deeply. "I'll have to call Dr. Flatley and let him take a look."

It was unbelievable, incomprehensible. Was I back on the same course I had been on only four months before?

By the time I got to the hospital I was shaking. I dreaded what Dr. Flatley would say.

"You should have known better!" he grumbled after he had examined me. "If you don't look after yourself, then who will, Jean? You're old enough to take responsibility for yourself."

Tears filled my eyes, but I didn't speak. The injustice of it all overwhelmed me. The truth was, I had no idea how this pressure sore had started. I had given up even trying to comprehend the humiliation and pain my body caused me. It had become my enemy, the thing I hated most.

Although the skin itself had only a small abrasion on it, the sore had tunneled underneath, going right down to the bone again. I was in for a repeat of the last operation: the muscle tissue removed from the back of my leg, the bead bed, the sitting up for ten minutes at a time—it was all the same. The whole experience left me feeling one hundred percent defeated.

When I got home two weeks later, I watched as Francie

preened in the mirror, went on dates, and worked a summer job. Meanwhile, up in our windowless attic room, I was stuck in bed, trying to keep any pressure off my bottom again. I spent many desperate hours debating whether or not to kill myself. A friend of Francie's had attempted to slit her wrists, and I thought that sounded fast and simple. So did swallowing a bunch of pills. In the end, though, I was too scared to follow through with the ideas.

By August, I was up and about in my wheelchair again, but I felt very vulnerable. I knew that my body could betray me at any moment, and I would be back in the hospital again. Over the summer, my parents had agreed that I could transfer to Custer High School, and I began to wonder what going to a public school would be like. I was hopeful that I'd be able to handle the work load better.

I thought, too, that arriving in a wheelchair might make it easier for a new group of students to accept me. I had always sensed that many of my classmates who knew me when I was walking were uncomfortable seeing me in a wheelchair.

As I had hoped, Custer High School was easier academically than Divine Savior Holy Angels High School. There were other changes, too. It was the first time I had been in a nonparochial school, and religion classes and Friday Mass were not part of the curriculum. Unlike at DSHA, where I had not known a single person in my grade when I started, I had many acquaintances from grade school at Custer. It was also the first time I had been in school alongside other disabled students.

Jim Ratzburg was one of two guys in wheelchairs. One day, soon after school began, he and I rolled up to use the elevator at the same time. It was only large enough for one wheelchair, so whoever pushed the button first got to go in first. "Hey, how's it going?" he said loudly.

I gave him a halfhearted smile. "All right," I said.

"What are you doing on Saturday?" He didn't even wait for a response. "Have you ever tried wheelchair soccer? I'm playing this Saturday. Do you want to come with me?"

"Wheelchair soccer?" I asked. "How do you do that? You need your legs to play soccer."

Jim shook his head. "It's this cool adapted game."

The word *adapted* set off flashing lights in my brain. "No, thanks," I mumbled. "I'm busy." I was relieved to see the elevator doors open and I rolled in. "See ya," I said, hoping I wouldn't.

In the time I had been at Custer High School, the other students had begun to group Jim and me together as a couple. One girl had even started a rumor that we were dating! This infuriated me. I had still not accepted the obvious reality that I was in a wheelchair. I reasoned that because I *could* easily get up and walk on crutches for short distances that I was not in the same category as Jim, who hardly ever used his crutches.

It was a minor distinction to most people, but it was one I clung to. Jim, too, had spina bifida, but his case appeared to be more severe than mine. Besides that, he was a big guy with a five o'clock shadow at eight o'clock in the morning. He also had a habit of using too much cologne. When I got into the elevator, I could

tell if Jim had beaten me to class by the amount of scent still waft-
ing around in there. Jim and I were alike in one way, though: We
both were very stubborn.

Jim wouldn't give up trying to get me to go to wheelchair soccer
with him. One day our paths crossed again outside the elevator. "I'm
serious. You should try wheelchair soccer. It's a blast," he said.

"Oh, come on," frustration edged into my voice. "You can't
play soccer without good legs."

"Of course you can," replied Jim. "You'd love it. It's adapted.
You just throw the ball instead of kicking it. Otherwise it's just the
same. And we play other sports, too. Come on and give it a try."

"No, I don't think so," I said as the elevator doors opened and I
wheeled inside. On the way down to the first floor I swore to myself
I would never get into anything as hokey as wheelchair sports. If I
was going to win it would be because I was good enough to win, and
not because I was in some special adapted sport.

Jim Ratzburg pestered me every week until I got tired of the
other students seeing him talking to me all the time. I decided I
would ask my mom if she would take me to one of the Saturday
morning soccer practices. Then I could tell Jim I had tried his
beloved sport and it wasn't for me. However, my mother told me
she had far too much housework to do to take me anywhere on
Saturday. This was even better. Now I had something concrete to
tell Jim. I could tell him I would go, but there was no way for me
to get across town to the gym where the practices were held.

I was hanging out in front of the school one lunch hour when
Jim came up beside me. "Well, are you going to go?" he asked me
yet again. "You know we are always looking for people."

"That's too bad," I said. "I want to come, but my mother says she's too busy to drive me there."

"My mom will take you," Jim replied eagerly.

My heart sank. I had painted myself into the proverbial corner. "Okay, I'll try it." I shrugged, thinking back to my original plan. I would go once, then tell Jim that wheelchair sports just didn't appeal to me.

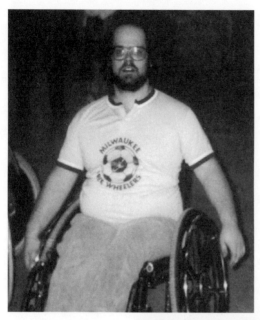

Top: Jim Ratzburg
introduced me to
wheelchair sports.

Bottom: Cindy Owens
coordinated the first
wheelchair sports
event I attended.

SEVEN

THE COOLEST THING
I'D EVER SEEN

When Saturday morning arrived, I did my usual chores of dusting and vacuuming the living room with a sense of impending dread. I was sorry I'd agreed to allow Jim Ratzburg and his mother to pick me up and take me to the silly games.

At 12:30 a big blue conversion van pulled into our driveway and an older, thin woman got out.

"Jean, your ride's here," yelled Jacques, who had been skate-boarding on the sidewalk.

"I know," I yelled back, annoyed that my brothers knew I was going somewhere with Jim. Using my crutches to walk, I grabbed the handles of my wheelchair to bring it along for the soccer game. I bounced it down the two steps from the stoop to the ground.

"You must be Jean. I'm Mrs. Ratzburg," said the woman. "Go ahead and get into the van while I put your chair in the back."

I nodded, too shy to speak, and walked up to the edge of the open side door. I placed my crutches into the van and pulled myself up onto the seat. Jim was in the front passenger seat.

"Hi," he greeted me. "Are you ready for some fun?"

"Yeah, I guess," I mumbled back nervously.

Thirty minutes later we were parking outside a recreation center owned by the Milwaukee County Parks System. Mrs. Ratzburg pulled our chairs out and unfolded them for us. Jim pulled the armrests out of his chair and left them in the van. I watched him enviously, wishing mine weren't welded into place.

I groaned inwardly when I got inside the building. It was exactly as I had feared it would be. A group of people sitting in manual and electric wheelchairs was starting a game of "baseball." *It's been adapted all right,* I told myself grimly as I noted the big plastic whiffle ball, small plastic bat, and T-ball stand. I glanced at my watch and calculated how much longer I would have to be there.

Jim introduced me to an energetic blonde named Cindy Owens. Cindy was the coordinator of the Milwaukee Public Schools Division of Recreation—Wheelchair Sports Program, and she had a great smile. After we had talked for a minute or two, she introduced me to Dale Garman, the coach of the sports teams.

"Glad to have you here," he said. "You can be on the green team."

I wheeled over and joined the team that was getting ready to bat. *I'm so embarrassed to be here,* I thought. *This is fine for kids who can't do anything else, but I sure don't need to be here.* I was so glad no one on this side of town knew me.

When it was my turn to bat, I whacked the ball as hard as I could. It whistled through the air.

"Great hit, Jean," yelled Dale, but I couldn't receive the compliment. I felt it was out of proportion to what I had done. I knew that it would have been an accomplishment for many of the players; they appeared to have very weak upper bodies, and some of them hardly had the strength to hit the plastic ball off the tee.

After about twenty minutes the plastic baseball game was over.

"We're going into the other gym now to play soccer. Dale will split you into teams again," Cindy announced.

"Are you ready to play, Jean?" asked Dale.

"Sure," I replied, imagining a plastic ball and a bunch of hesitant players.

When we got into the gym I could see guys but no other girls in manual wheelchairs. One of the boys, who was a little younger than me, had the coolest wheelchair. It was smaller than mine and had a frame painted candy-apple red, with no armrests. *Now that's one sporty chair,* I told myself, knowing it had to be way out of my family's budget.

The two teams lined up and a big red rubber ball was thrown into the center. There were goal nets six feet high and six feet wide at each end of the court. Each goal was guarded by two goalies.

Oh, brother. Here we go again, I thought, wishing I'd never agreed to get involved.

The whistle blew, and I watched as two manual wheelchairs came whizzing down the court from opposite ends toward the ball. Crash! They whammed into each other. The player on the left was catapulted out of his chair and onto the court. I waited to hear the whistle blow and see an able-bodied person run out to rescue the guy on the floor, but it never happened. Instead the other player grabbed the ball and started bouncing it down the court past me. A college-aged man swiveled his wheelchair around and grabbed the ball. Another player swooped in and pulled it out of his hands, lobbing it down the court.

I sat there riveted. This was the coolest thing I had ever seen! These guys were really playing hard. Every turnover was vigorously contested, and every goal hard fought.

"Wow," I yelled as much to myself as to anyone else. I was elated that I had finally found something competitive I could do, something as rough and tumble as any sport I'd ever seen. *I'd better watch what I'm doing out here!*

**The player on the left was catapulted
out of his chair and onto the court.**

I rolled down the court beside a player from the other team who had the ball. I veered into his chair, hoping to throw him off balance enough so that I could grab the ball. Getting in on the action felt great. By halftime, I was hooked.

During the second half I got thrown out of my chair twice. The first time, I had the ball and looked up to see an electric chair bearing down on me at full speed. I spotted one of my team members out of the corner of my eye and heaved the ball toward him. A cheer went up from the coach. I laughed out loud. This was such fun!

When the game was over, I rolled over to the sideline.

"Hey, you're good!" said Cindy. "You're coming back next week, aren't you?"

"I hope so!" I replied, wiping the sweat off my face with the back of my sleeve.

"We've got other activities going on this summer too. Have you even been water-skiing?" she asked.

I giggled. Water-skiing? Was there really a way I could go water-skiing? I supposed she knew what she was talking about. "No, but I'd like to," I said. Actually, *love* to would have more accurately summed up how I felt. I remembered when the next-door neighbors had invited Ray to go water-skiing with them. I had been so jealous.

"Well, we'll put you on the list. If you give me your phone number and address, I can send you brochures on all the wheelchair sports and events we're offering over the summer," said Cindy.

"Would you?" I asked. The phrase *wheelchair sports* had a whole new meaning now that I had actually played a game of wheelchair soccer.

"Sure," she said. "And we have different activities in winter. We work with the Center for Independent Living, and they offer ice hockey. That's fun to play."

"Ice hockey? On ice?" I asked, hearing how dumb my question sounded as I said it.

"Sure, why not?" Cindy replied. "There's a ton of cool sports out there. We have lots of fun, but it's serious, too. People want their teams to win, believe me."

I smiled. I had no trouble believing her! This was turning out to be one of the most liberating days of my life.

When Mrs. Ratzburg arrived, I was reluctant to go home. As I climbed back into the van, I examined my wheelchair. It hadn't fared too well. I could see a crack in one of the welds holding the brake mechanism and both the footplates were crooked. But I liked the new roughed-up look. Anyone examining my chair could see I didn't stay on the sidelines all the time.

As the sports continued, so did the deterioration of my chair. It was falling apart from the abuse I was giving it. Three more welds cracked and the footplates were chipped, twisted, and beat up. Still, it didn't enter my mind that my parents would care until one night after soccer when I went home with my brake in my hand. It had broken off my chair.

"Just look at your wheelchair, Jean!" my mother scolded. "You're going to have to stop playing sports. We can't afford three hundred dollars for a new one. It's just getting too banged up."

"But, Mom…"

"No. I'm not arguing with you. No more sports," she said.

The next day I told Jim Ratzburg not to bother picking me up anymore. I wasn't allowed to participate.

He looked shocked, but I didn't want to tell him the details.

On Saturday morning the phone rang. I heard my mother answer it. I could tell immediately she was talking about me. I tried not to listen, but I gathered it was Cindy from the wheelchair sports program. They talked for a long time, and when she got off the phone, Mom came into the living room to talk to me.

"That was the woman from the wheelchair sports," she said.

"Really?" I replied. "What did you two talk about?"

"Well, she wanted to know why you aren't allowed to go anymore, and I explained to her that your chair was getting too banged up."

"Oh," I said, hoping that wasn't the end of the conversation.

"She said they need you on the teams and that the program will take full responsibility for your chair. If it gets too bad, they'll replace it."

"And what did you say?" I asked, bursting with hope.

Mom took a long look at me. "When you've finished the vacuuming you can call Mrs. Ratzburg and tell her to pick you up this afternoon if you like."

I wanted to reach over and hug her, but instead I just said thank you.

Over the next several months I tried out every sport I could.

As I sat there on the floor to vacuum as I typically did (the wheelchair took up too much room with the vacuum), I ran through all the activities that I intended to try over the next few months. Number one on my list of sports to try was water-skiing, and it proved to be even more fun than I had imagined. A group of us went to a lake in Thiensville, about twenty-five miles north of Milwaukee. Instead of two skis, we used one long ski that looked like a surfboard with a notch at the front for the rope and supported a small aluminum cage to sit in. When it was my turn, I jumped into the water and grabbed the board. I then forced it under me and found my balance. After that I adjusted my legs so they were tucked up under my chest and held on to the bar. I gave the driver a thumbs-up, and the motor roared into gear.

It took me several tries before I could stay up on my own, but eventually I got the hang of it. Water-skiing was so different from anything else I had ever done, and I loved skimming across the lake at full speed. I wasn't brave enough the first time to attempt jumping over the boat's wake, but I couldn't wait for the next outing. Maybe I would try it then.

Over the next several months I tried out every sport I could. Mrs. Ratzburg picked me up each time she took Jim to play. Tennis proved to be a disaster; I swung the racket with such gusto the ball sailed over the back fence nearly every time. Ice hockey was much more fun. I had wondered how a wheelchair could get any traction on ice but I soon found out that the games were held after an able-bodied team finished practicing, so the ice was scuffed up. Most of the wheelchair hockey players used mountain bike–style tires too. The rules stipulated that no one was allowed to raise his or her stick above knee height, but in the heat of the moment sticks often went flying. Some players careened across the ice after being thrown out of their chairs; others stayed in their chairs but skidded into the boards.

Sometimes I got thrown around or hit with a stick while fighting for the puck. But I didn't even give a thought to the potential for injury. I was totally caught up in the exhilaration of playing a competitive sport. Since my hip was already dislocated again (and is to this day!), I didn't have to worry about that.

My love of sports continued to grow throughout my senior year of high school. I didn't have any pressure sores or major injuries that year, either, though I did take two weeks off from school to have an artificial valve inserted into my bladder so that I could better control its function. Although it took several frustrating months of adjustments to get the valve to work correctly, it was worth the effort. For the first time since sixth grade, I didn't have a urine bag strapped to my leg. It felt wonderful. I bought a denim skirt to celebrate!

As my graduation date grew near, I faced the inevitable question: What was I going to do with the rest of my life? From as early as I could remember, my mother had told me she thought my best career choice would be to become a secretary. It was an obvious choice, because the job requires a lot of sitting. Inside, I rebelled against this idea. I didn't want a job that could be "adapted" for my needs; I wanted a chance at whatever career I chose.

I decided I wanted to be a nurse. Ever since I had been in the hospital for the series of hip surgeries, I'd had my heart set on it. The nurses had become my best friends. In fact, I still kept in touch with about ten of them. At times their sense of humor was the only thing that kept me going, and I wanted to provide that kind of support to other children who found themselves in similar situations.

I told my mother about my career choice, but she wasn't encouraging.

"How are you going to lift patients or turn them in bed?" she asked.

"I'll get help if I need it," I replied, remembering how the nurses worked in teams at the hospital.

"But what if no one is around?" she countered.

"Well, I'll wait until someone shows up. Mom, you're only thinking of the one thing I might have trouble with. Think of all the things I could do perfectly fine. I could weigh people, take their blood pressure, give them shots, and hand out pills."

"Be realistic," Mom said, shaking her head. "Think it through, Jean. Stick with something within your capabilities."

I opened my mouth to say more, but I didn't. It was hard for me, a teenager, to talk to my mother about things that really mattered to me. I *had* thought it through. Kids with spina bifida and similar conditions were in and out of the hospital all the time, and I could only imagine the encouragement it would give them to see a nurse in a wheelchair. Besides, I'd been working with kids all my life. I had baby-sat for years and I'd always found a way to do what needed to be done.

I graduated right on schedule on June 8, 1984, one year behind Francie. I had made mostly *A*s and *B*s in my classes, and I was glad to be done with high school forever. By then Mom had given up arguing with me, and I enrolled as a prenursing major at the University of Wisconsin—Milwaukee.

I lived at home because it was cheaper, and a van service took me to college and back each day. What had started out as a dream, though, quickly disintegrated into a nightmare. On a crisp night in early spring, a police officer arrived at our door to serve divorce papers to my father.

He was shocked. I was shocked. All my siblings were shocked. I knew my parents had problems. They had been to counseling and they didn't seem to talk to each other much, but I had no idea their marriage was that close to the edge. My father moved out, and both he and my mother began leaning on us children for loyalty and support. The effect this had on my already fragile sense of self was devastating. I found I couldn't concentrate on my classwork. I spent hours beating myself up emotionally because I thought that in some way I had contributed to the divorce. Money had always been an issue in our family, and I knew I had used up far more than my portion. I was responsible for high medical insurance costs and exorbitant medical bills, many of which were not covered by insurance, not to mention the cost of my wheelchair and braces. *Did* this *make me responsible for their divorce?* I wondered.

The only time I felt really free of my torment was when I was playing sports. I signed up to participate in every sport I could find, until I was out every night of the week. I continued to go to my classes—English, basic algebra, psychology, and anatomy and physiology—but I was barely keeping my head above water. I berated myself mercilessly. Maybe I wasn't good enough to make it at college after all. By the time the year was over, I was on academic probation. The dean gave me the fall semester of 1985 to pull myself together.

That summer I set my sights on getting my driver's license and a car. My mother felt that it made more sense for me to have my own car than for her to have hand controls added to hers.

Mom called around and found the Curative Rehabilitation Hospital, which offered driving courses for people with disabilities. Some people needed vans with electric lifts. I just needed a car with hand controls to practice in. I signed up for twice-weekly lessons over the summer. To get to Curative, I took a city bus to Wisconsin

Avenue and transferred to a Watertown–Plank Road bus. The
buses had no wheelchair lifts, so I used my crutches instead. I
would clamber off the bus at the bottom of a steep hill. Curative was
at the top. The walk may have seemed short to some, but it took all
my energy to get to the top of that hill. Yet it was worth every ounce
of effort to get there. I longed for the freedom that being able to
drive and having my own car would give me.

**I longed for the freedom that being able to
drive and having my own car would give me.**

I took to the hand controls quickly. They weren't hard to operate at all. Both the brake and the accelerator pedals had poles
bolted to their arms that were attached to a single handle on the
left side of the steering column. To accelerate I pushed the handle
down toward my lap; to slow down or stop I pushed it toward the
dash. By the end of the first lesson I had these controls mastered
and was ready to tackle parallel parking and lane changing.

Mom offered to cosign a two-thousand-dollar loan for me to
cover the cost of the 1978 maroon Cutlass Supreme I picked out.
Brian, one of my soccer friends, went with me to buy the hand-
control conversion kit and to install it for me. I was ready to hit the
road!

The day I bought the car was a milestone for me. Now I
would no longer be dependent on my mother or my friends to
drive me places. I could come and go as I pleased. Although I
could not yet work for a living, Social Security helped me pay
many of my own bills.

By the time the fall semester started I was feeling much more optimistic. For one thing, I had arranged to move into a dorm on campus. I hoped this would help me to make new friends and leave the stress of home behind. However, my father felt freer to visit me now that I was not living at home with my mother. Lonely and confused, he often stopped by, looking to me for support and consolation. I was so upset by the disintegration of my family, however, that I had little to offer him.

By midsemester, I couldn't take it anymore. I had no idea why I couldn't concentrate on my coursework, nor did I have any idea where to turn to talk about it. Finally, one Thursday evening, I called my Aunt Joan for a chat. We started talking about the trips my uncle, a truck driver, had recently taken. Without warning I burst into sobs. I was as startled as Aunt Joan must have been. I had learned early in life never to let other people see my hurts. Aunt Joan asked what the problem was, and all the frustration of my wheelchair, my poor grades, my family problems, and my profound sense of failure came spilling out.

My roommate walked in and then tiptoed out again. I cried and talked for two hours, going back over everything from my low grades to the perverseness of God in making me so imperfect.

When it was over I tried to tell myself I felt better, but I didn't. The cork was out of the bottle now. If I wanted to stay at college, I knew I had to find some new way to cope with the lot life had given me.

As it happened, the decision of what to do next was taken out of my hands. Later that semester I developed yet another dreaded pressure sore, requiring another operation and hospital stay.

Three days after the operation, while I was still trying to come to terms with this latest surgery and my emotional meltdown, Mom came to visit me. She brought my mail. The first letter had the University of Wisconsin seal on it. I opened it warily. "Dear Jean," I read, "We regret to inform you that you have not met the requirements needed in order to continue your studies at the University of Wisconsin—Milwaukee. You are ineligible for readmission for the spring semester of 1986. If you have any questions, or feel this step has been taken in error, please respond in writing to..."

I felt as if I had just been thumped in the stomach.

"What is it, Jean?" my mother asked.

I handed her the letter.

"Oh," she said after scanning it. "So it's that bad."

"Yeah," I replied. "It's that bad."

Suddenly the shame of failure overwhelmed me. I knew I would die if anyone found out I had flunked out of college. I turned to my mother. "Mom, please, please don't tell anyone. Promise you won't say why I'm leaving college, not to anyone, not even to Aunt Joan."

My mother looked at me. "Okay, I won't," she replied. "But you had better figure out some way to get your life together."

Top: The O'Briens helped me move in a new direction.

Bottom: I continued trying every sport I could.

New Direction

"I am a C. I am a C-H. I am a C-H-R-I-S-T-I-A-N."

I turned my head into the pillow and groaned. It was Lori O'Brien again, one of the young LPNs in the ward. It was 6 A.M. and she was checking my vital signs, singing and laughing as she did so. It wasn't the first time she had awakened me with her trite little songs. I would have found Lori's religious fervor intolerable if it were not for the fact that she had a great sense of humor. Also, unlike some of the other nurses, she wasn't constantly harassing me about why I didn't take care of my body.

When she finished the chorus, she started on a rousing round of "Rise and Shine, and Give God the Glory, Glory" as she shook out the thermometer and tightened the blood pressure cuff around my arm.

"So what are you going to do when you get home?" she asked brightly.

"I don't know." I hated to be reminded that, though I had no idea what it was, my life was about to take some drastic new direction. I felt totally out of control, like a passenger on some nightmarish ride. Passing the courses at college should have been well within my reach, but I had been sideswiped both by my parents' divorce and by all the bottled-up anger I still felt about being stuck in a wheelchair.

I lay on the bead bed for another week before I was allowed to go home. I could hardly stand to see any of my old friends. My insecurities convinced me that they were saying, "See, everyone was right. Jean doesn't have what it takes to be a nurse." I lost all my enthusiasm for life. The only thing I wanted to do was to get back to sports. Unfortunately, I still had a long road of recovery ahead of me before that would be possible.

My mother kept telling me I needed to get on with my life, but how? All of my dreams were dead.

About a week after I got home, Lori called to see how I was doing. I must have sounded as depressed as I felt because she made me an offer. "How about you come and live with us for a year? I want to go back to school and become a registered nurse and that means Dan is going to have to work twelve to fourteen hours a day to bring in enough money to keep us afloat. We need a nanny. How about it?" she asked.

I didn't know what to say. On the one hand, I wasn't going back to college, and I wanted to find some way to get out of the house. On the other hand, did I want to live with someone who sang Christian choruses at all hours of the day and night?

"Well?" she prodded. "You've met Danny and Naomi, and you know how much fun they are!"

I had never thought about being a live-in nanny before, but it sounded like a good idea.

"Sure," I replied. "When can I come over and talk about it?"

The next afternoon I drove over to Lori's home in West Allis, by the State Fair grounds. Three-year-old Naomi and fifteen-month-old Danny were waiting at the door for me.

I moved in with the O'Brien family a week later, on January 24, 1986. I quickly adjusted to the nanny routine. People often looked at me quizzically when I wheeled into the neighborhood park with the two children in my lap. Sometimes another mom or babysitter would try to help me with the kids, though I had everything under control. Even though these well-meaning people would not have believed it, being in a wheelchair didn't make nannying much more complicated than it would have been had I been able to walk.

At the house, I would get out of my wheelchair and sit on the floor to play LEGOs with the children. I dressed Danny in his little denim overalls and brushed Naomi's hair and put pretty barrettes in it. I made their meals and supervised Danny as he plastered food all over his face. I read books to them, and I tucked them in for their naps with a hug and a kiss.

Admittedly, some tasks were a little more complicated, but I had found ways around doing things the "normal" way since I was young. For instance, to take Danny up or down the stairs, I would put him on my back in his backpack carrier and walk up by holding on to the railing and using a crutch to steady me. When it was time to hang out the laundry, I would put the basket on the wooden picnic table and drag it, little by little, across the yard under the clothesline, using it to sit on as I hung out the clothes.

When Lori first asked me to be a nanny, I figured that I would probably be expected to attend church with the family. This left me with a tight feeling in my stomach. I'd been force-fed enough religion and attended enough faith-healing meetings to last me a lifetime. I remembered the time when I was fifteen and my parents had dragged me off to a revival and healing meeting in Milwaukee. The preacher there had gathered a huge crowd of well over two thousand people. We came in late and had to sit near the back. I watched expectantly as the preacher selected people out of the audience that he said God wanted to heal.

There was one woman in the third row whom he prayed for loudly, casting out a demon of sickle cell anemia, and an old man whose leg he prayed over to be lengthened. As I studied what was happening, hope welled up within me. If God had healed them, then surely he could heal me! However, the preacher never came near the back of the auditorium, so I didn't have the opportunity to be prayed for. My parents told me that they would bring me back much earlier the following evening, and I jumped at the chance. All the next day I fantasized about being cured of my spina bifida. I thought about every word the preacher had said. I had been told by well-meaning people that if a sick person had enough faith, God would honor that faith and heal him or her. But if a person doubted even one tiny bit, God would see that and withhold healing.

I tried desperately to rid myself of any hint of doubt. Instead I envisioned the new, healed me. There would be no more weak legs, no more crutches, no more wheelchair! I could hardly wait. By dinnertime, the three of us were lined up outside the revival meeting, determined to secure a spot within praying distance of the evangelist.

When we got to the eighth row from the front I was ecstatic. Surely the preacher would see me there and all my problems would be gone. I was sitting still, taking in the scene about half an hour before the meeting was scheduled to begin, when I saw the preacher himself emerge from a side door. He approached a heavy-set black woman sitting in a wheelchair in the same row as I was, on the aisle that ran down to the stage. She was within easy earshot of me and although the preacher talked softly, I could hear every word they said.

"Welcome in the name of Jesus the healer," he said.

"Oh my. Oh my," said the woman, obviously overcome with the shock of meeting such an important man.

"What are you seeking healing for tonight, sister?"

"What are you seeking healing for tonight, sister?" the evangelist asked.

"Oh," she replied. "Praise the Lord! I need a touch for my rheumatoid arthritis. The doctor says it's the worst case he's ever seen. But Jesus can heal me."

"Amen, sister," he replied, patting her on the arm. "Believe it. Receive it. Jesus is going to heal you tonight."

Tingling excitement shot through me. "God," I prayed, "don't forget me."

The preacher moved farther down the row, out of earshot. I watched as he spoke to several other people, then disappeared back behind the side door.

Soon organ music began and the gathered crowd stood and sang, "He is Lord, he is Lord, he is risen from the dead and he is Lord."

When the music faded away, the preacher made his official entrance.

"Praise God," he began. "Say amen if you're looking for a miracle at the hands of Jesus tonight!"

A chorus of amens went up from the crowd.

"Well, let's see what the Lord will do." He stepped down off the stage and onto the main floor. "I sense there is a woman here who is deeply troubled. She has been tormented with an affliction. I see it. I understand, Jesus. Yes, it's rheumatoid arthritis. Oh Lord, it's the worst case the doctor has ever seen."

He walked toward my row. "I believe our sister is in this row. Here she is." He walked up to the woman I had heard him talking to before the service. "Sister, tell us, are you the one the Lord wants to heal of rheumatoid arthritis tonight?"

"Oh, hallelujah. Yes, Jesus. I claim the victory," the woman said.

"And sister what is your name?"

"Beulah."

"And have we ever spoken before, Beulah?"

"No sir," she said.

"Never?"

"No, never," Beulah replied.

"And did the doctor tell you you've got the worst case he's ever seen?"

"Yes, brother. Amen, brother. Praise God, he's healing me," she replied.

I turned to look back at the audience. All around the auditorium people were nodding in agreement, raising their hands to God and praying. Loathing gripped my stomach as I processed what I was hearing. The preacher went down the row praying for other people, but now instead of wanting him to pray for me I hoped he wouldn't come near me. He didn't, and I left the auditorium with my faith shattered. I never again wanted to go into a revival meeting or be prayed for. As far as I was concerned, everything about Christianity was as fake as that healing meeting.

I was far too uncomfortable to tell Lori O'Brien my views on religion. It just seemed easier to me to go along with her to church and not make waves. The first time I went to church with the family I felt awkward and out of place. I didn't know any of the songs, which everyone else appeared to know by heart. I couldn't find my way around the Bible either. I had read bits of it for my confirmation class, but I was shocked by the way these church members carried their Bibles with them to church and eagerly looked up passages as the pastor spoke. It seemed fanatical to me.

After a few Sundays, the whole experience became less intimidating, and I began to relax a little, though I promised myself I would never be one of "them."

I continued to throw myself into my wheelchair sports in the evenings. I had some money left over from a college fund my grandparents had set up for me. Since I would no longer need it for college, I decided to treat myself to a proper sports wheelchair. The one I settled on had a narrow, bright yellow aluminum frame with no armrests and small footplates. It cost thirteen hundred dollars, but to me it was worth every cent. Since it weighed only twenty-three pounds it was easy for me to lift in and out of the car, and it was fast! I soon grew to like being referred to as the "fast girl in the yellow chair."

By now Cindy Owens and I had become good friends, and I often helped her with mailings for upcoming events. I also competed in every sports event I could.

In the spring, Cindy told me she was organizing a seminar for wheelchair athletes. The guest speakers were to be Dr. Brad and Sharon Hedrick. I knew their names well. Dr. Brad Hedrick was the supervisor of the Recreation and Athletics Program for Students with Disabilities at the University of Illinois. Sharon, now a registered nutritionist, had been the first person in a wheelchair ever to win a gold medal at the Olympic Games, where wheelchair racing was an exhibition sport.

Oddly enough, I remembered watching Sharon on television the day she won. The TV wasn't normally on during the day at our house, but for some reason my father was watching the Olympics on that particular day of the wheelchair events. I stopped dead in my tracks and leaned on my crutches when I saw the women's 800-meter race start. I watched as Sharon Hedrick rolled across the finish line in first place. I was impressed.

"Hey, I want to do that someday," I said to my dad.

He looked at me. "Jean, that's a bit out of your league, don't you think?"

I wanted to retort, "No, I don't see why I couldn't do that," but I decided to keep my mouth shut. I didn't want to share any more of my dreams, because every time I let my guard down and did so, someone would tell me why I couldn't achieve them. I was tired of listening to negative statements. However, I would always remember seeing Sharon Hedrick cross the finish line in her wheelchair, and I was eager to meet her and her husband in person.

As it happened, Sharon got sick and was unable to teach at the seminar, so Brad delivered her lecture about good nutrition for the athlete. When the seminar was finished he stayed to watch an exhibition game of soccer that Cindy had organized. It was a hot and furious game, and I thought I made several good moves. When I was finished, Brad came up to me. "That was quite a game you played, young lady," he said.

There was a huge rivalry between Wisconsin and Illinois, and I wasn't about to be a traitor.

"Thanks," I replied, grinning from ear to ear.

Brad continued. "How would you like to be a member of the University of Illinois women's wheelchair basketball team? I have a spot in the program just for you!"

"Oh, well…," I sputtered, not quite knowing what to say. This was the last thing I had expected.

"You'll love it there!" he went on. "We've got the best coaches anywhere, and you would have the opportunity to travel throughout the country, competing in regional and national events."

"Ah," I said, trying to sound interested, though in my heart I was sure I would never move to Illinois. After all there was a huge rivalry between Wisconsin and Illinois, and I wasn't about to be a traitor. I wasn't rude enough to say it, but I was sure Illinois had nothing to offer me. I politely said, "Thanks very much for the offer. Let me think about it."

"Sure," said Brad, reaching down for his briefcase. He pulled out a notebook and pen. "Write down your name and address, and I'll send you some information just in case."

"Okay. I'll look forward to receiving the information," I lied.

A week later Brad sent me an information packet from the University of Illinois, then he followed it up with a phone call. Every couple of weeks from then on, I either received something in the mail or got a call from Brad. Even though I had no intention of signing up for the program at Illinois, it was very flattering to be so heavily recruited. My confession about my previous problems at college didn't even daunt Brad. "Just tell me you'll come, and we'll find a way to get you here," he would say.

Throughout the summer I went on with my life as a nanny. I played sports in the evenings, and on the weekends I went to parties or to the bar with my friends. Then in November, something subtle happened that did not have many immediate repercussions in my life. I had been attending an Assemblies of God church with the O'Briens for eleven months. Although much of it was still very foreign to me, I found myself listening to what the pastor had to say.

Over time, the bitterness and disappointment that I felt toward God because I was not healed began to recede. I found myself softening to the idea that God really did love me and that he alone could give me a peace and purpose. However, after all the healing services I had attended with my parents I wasn't interested in doing anything showy or public about it. Instead, one night in November 1986, I prayed quietly in my room and asked God to forgive me for my sins, whatever they were, and to come into my heart.

I doubt if Lori or anyone else saw much of a change in me. I didn't start talking about what I had done or reading my Bible regularly or anything else like that. Yet inside I had the sense that I was now a child of God.

About the same time, I grew restless with being a nanny. Lori was expecting another baby, and if I stayed beyond my year's commitment I would be looking after an infant as well as the other two children. While I loved kids, I was just twenty years old and wanted desperately to find my own niche in the world. Live-in nannying, I decided, wasn't it.

As Brad Hedrick's letters and phone calls piled in, I began to give serious thought to going to the University of Illinois. After all, no one had ever wanted me that much before! I began to think that I could make it as a college athlete and full-time student. So in November, I filled out the necessary forms and returned them to the school.

I had told Brad all along that my college transcripts from the University of Wisconsin—Milwaukee were not good, and I wasn't surprised when the University of Illinois turned down my application. They weren't convinced I could handle the course load.

They did give me one opportunity to prove myself, however. If I could get accepted back into my previous university and pass a full course load for a semester, they would then accept me at the

University of Illinois. It was one more hurdle, but once I had made up my mind to go to Illinois, I set about overcoming it. I wrote a letter to my former dean, explaining the reasons for my breakdown and poor grades the year before and asking him for another chance. He gave it to me, and I enrolled in the School of Allied Health, where I took twelve credit hours of general courses.

I moved back home and worked hard, determined to stay on the right track this time. By May 1987 I had passed all of my courses with *B*s and *C*s, I was looking forward to participating in some exciting wheelchair sports events during summer, and I was preparing to go to Champaign, Illinois, in the fall.

Jim Derse bought my first racing chair and my first plane ticket.

Ann Cody (on left) and me at my first national track meet.

NINE

ILLINOIS AT LAST

In May 1987 the regional games were held in Milwaukee. I was extremely nervous, not only because of the competition but also because I was going to meet Marty Morse, the track coach for the University of Illinois. Since basketball and wheelchair racing were the sports the university was best known for, I figured he and I would most likely be working closely together in the years ahead. Professionally, I knew he was the best. His reputation as one of the top wheelchair track coaches in the world preceded him. He had coached Sharon Hedrick to the Olympic gold medal. On a personal level, I liked him instantly. He was also in a wheelchair, the result of an accident while riding his motocross bike at nineteen years of age. Marty had a warm personality and an encouraging way about him. I was flattered when he expressed excitement over my impending move to Illinois.

In June, I went to Houston, Texas, for the U.S. National Wheelchair Games. I had met the qualifying times in both swimming and track, the sports I had focused on in Milwaukee. I had one man to thank for my being at the games. His name was Jim Derse, and he had been on the board of the Easter Seals Society in

Milwaukee for many years. The year before I had also qualified for
the National Wheelchair Games, but I hadn't been able to afford
to go. I didn't know it at the time, but when Jim Derse learned that
I hadn't had the money to go, he called Cindy Owens. He told her
that if anyone from Milwaukee qualified for nationals again and
was unable to go because of a lack of funds, his foundation would
make up the difference.

Jim was true to his word, and his foundation paid for my first
racing chair and all my expenses so I could compete in events
across the country.

I was thrilled to have someone who believed in me, and I was
determined to do my best at the national games. Unfortunately, in
Houston the track and swimming competitions were held at the
same time, so I was forced to choose which event I wanted to debut
in. It wasn't a hard decision to reach. Since I only weighed a hundred pounds, my body didn't have much insulation, and I hated
diving into cold pools. I chose track, signing up for all the sprinting events—the 100 meters, 200 meters, 400 meters, and 800
meters—along with the slalom course. The slalom is a particularly
challenging event, much like an obstacle course, in which athletes
have to reverse and spin between cones, push over a ladder laying
on the ground, and race up and down steep ramps.

I had done some training in preparation for the meet, swimming timed laps and sprinting out on the track in my racing chair.
I loved the challenge of trying to go faster on each sprint than I had
on the one before. And while I hadn't trained as vigorously as many
of the other athletes in my field, I had the golden touch in Houston. I won every event I entered, netting five gold medals and a

place on the U.S. Developmental Wheelchair Track and Field Team. The team would be going to the Stoke–Mandeville Games in Aylesbury, England, northwest of London, in July.

My family had no grasp of the level of competitive sports I was working my way into. Wheelchair sports were an unfamiliar world to them. When I arrived home from Houston, I showed Mom my medals. "Good job," she said, admiring them for a moment. "But you missed doing your Saturday chores. You have vacuuming to do." On her only day off, Mom was intent on getting things done.

She was impressed, though, when I told her I had won a spot on the team going to England and even more so when I told her there were no money concerns associated with the trip. Once again, Jim Derse's foundation generously came to my aid, providing two thousand dollars to cover my airfare and accommodations.

I could hardly believe how my life was turning around. Wheelchair sports had provided me with something to really sink my teeth into, something I was proud to be a part of.

I should have been totally focused on winning in England, but I found myself distracted by Dave, player number six on the developmental U.S. basketball team. He was tall and blond. I was twenty years old and desperately wanted to be like every other girl I knew, going on dates and having boyfriends. Dave was appealing to me, so for the ten days I was in England, Dave and I were an "item." Fortunately, despite the distraction, I came in first in every event I entered. I even won the title Queen of the Straight, which was given to the fastest woman in the 100 meters event.

Coach Marty Morse was a little concerned about my relationship with Dave. He took me aside and talked to me about how he expected me to be a serious athlete and how I should keep myself free of distractions while at the University of Illinois. Not that guys were out of the question, but I had to be protective of my time. I was beginning to see that being on a coach-affiliated university team was a serious commitment, one that would take all of my effort to fulfill.

For the first time the media began to pay attention to me, not as a poster child with a disability but as a real athlete. A reporter and photographer from the *Milwaukee Journal* came to do an article on me. I proudly posed with all nine medals from the games in England hanging around my neck.

On August 23, 1987, Ron Zima, a friend from the Spina Bifida Association, pulled into the driveway in a black pickup truck. He was there to load up my belongings and help me move to Illinois.

When everything was finally crammed into the back of his truck, I said good-bye to my mother and Jacques, who was the only child still living at home at that time, and got into my 1978 Cutlass Supreme. In convoy formation, Ron and I headed south on the interstate out of Milwaukee. In about two and a half hours, the rolling hills gave way to the monotony of the flat prairie. Before long there was hardly a tree in sight, just rows and rows of soybean plants and cornstalks as far as the eye could see. My heart sank as I thought back to the beauty of Wisconsin and my friends and family. I wondered how long I could stand the tedium of living in the middle of acres of corn. I felt as if I had been transported back into the musical *Oklahoma!* "Where the wind comes sweeping down the plain..."

As I gazed out the window I thought about what I wanted from the coming school year. It came down to two things. First, I promised myself I would keep my grades up in every course. Second, I would do everything in my power to avoid another pressure sore and the hospital time that involved.

I was anxious as we pulled onto the campus of the university but was quickly relieved to find one familiar face. My new roommate, Ronda Jarvis, was already unpacking her things in our dorm room. I had met her at a sports camp at the University of Illinois early in the summer. We'd hit it off right away.

"Hi," Ronda said, smiling. "I'm so sorry my stuff is all over the place."

"Oh, that's okay," I replied.

"I got here yesterday," she went on, "and all I've managed to do is spread my stuff from one end of the room to the other. It's a pretty small room, but then what dorm room isn't?" She laughed.

I laughed too. It was so good to be on my own. I just *had* to find a way to make my new life work.

From the first meeting I had on campus with Marty Morse, I knew my days would be busy. We planned my classes so that I would start early in the morning and be done by midday or one o'clock at the latest. Then I would be off to the gym.

Marty gave me a tour of the Rehabilitation Education Center, the place where I would spend many hours training. One of the first things he showed me in the gym was a roller. This contraption consisted of a three-foot-wide drum and a frame. The front end of my racing chair would be clamped to the frame, and the back wheels would spin freely in place on the drum. Being on the roller was much like being a hamster on a wheel. You could go as fast as you liked, but you'd never get anywhere. I would begin using the device in November.

The front of my racing wheelchair sported a Cateye brand cyclo-computer, which told me how fast I was going, as well as my time, average speed, distance, maximum speed and total distance during each workout. I was thrilled when I could sustain thirteen to fourteen miles an hour. Marty, however, thought I could do better.

When my time on the rollers was up, I had to report to Brad Hedrick, the basketball coach. I soon found out that my understanding of the way basketball is played was woefully inadequate. Brad, who had a Ph.D. in leisure studies, was incredibly patient with me and several of the other newcomers. He had to go back to the beginning, explaining to us how to "read" the basketball floor and ways to predict what was going to happen next. I was too short to be considered seriously as an offensive player, but I loved playing defense. Scrambling for a loose ball got my adrenaline pumping!

About a week into my time at Illinois, Marty took Ann Cody and me out for a road workout. Although Ann was the national champion in the 1,500- and 5,000-meter events, I had beaten her in the 800-meter race in Houston. That, along with my other wins in England, had left me feeling pretty confident about my ability to keep up with her—far too confident as it turned out. We all headed out across campus. Our destination was three miles east of the rehab center, where Marty had measured out a four-mile practice loop. By the time we began the actual workout I was already tired. One lap and several sprints later I was exhausted. While Marty and Ann looked as fresh as when we left the campus, I was ready for a break!

"Okay. Let's go another lap!" shouted Marty.

Marty "took the pull," which meant that Ann and I would stay in his draft. This practice of drafting is similar to the technique competitive bicyclists use. The person in front works the hardest, breaking through the wind for those who follow. In wheelchair racing, good sportsmanship dictates that all the members in a pack take their turn at the head of the line. A person riding in the draft of someone else does about 30 percent less work than the person in front.

"We'll continue with one-minute sprints," Marty yelled back at us. I groaned inside. I was ready for a rest, not a sprint. I pushed hard on my wheels as Marty sped up to about seventeen miles per hour for a minute, slowed down to about twelve miles per hour for a minute, then moved up to seventeen again. After about five of these intervals, Ann took the lead and sprinted for a minute before falling back in line. I knew it was my turn next. I summoned all my energy and pulled hard for the minute, then dropped back. However, the next time my turn came around I couldn't find the energy to sprint. I dropped back, struggling to keep up with the others.

By the end of the workout, I was well behind. There was no way I could keep up with Marty and Ann's sprint times. I could barely keep up when they slowed down. I felt totally deflated. I knew Marty placed a lot of emphasis on endurance and stamina, and it was obvious I had very little of it. In the past I had done only the things that came more easily to me. Now I dreaded the long workouts I knew lay ahead. While Marty was training me for sprinting, he also suggested he would like to see me doing some longer races with Ann. I adamantly refused. I couldn't imagine anything worse than racing for 1,500 or 5,000 meters.

As the semester progressed, most of the time I felt as if I was split down the middle. I knew I would be thrown out of the athletics program if I didn't keep up my grades, but that involved a lot of work. I would rush to class, cram for tests between practices, and do my research assignments blurry-eyed at five o'clock in the morning. Everything I did had to fit around six or seven basketball practices a week, my weight training, time on the rollers, and trying to keep up with Marty's road and track endurance workouts. All this left me with about seven hours a night to sleep and no time at all for any kind of social activity. I hardly got to know a single person who wasn't associated with wheelchair sports. I missed my social life, but there was nothing I could do about it. I'd made a commitment to Brad Hedrick, much as I regretted it sometimes, and I was determined not to flunk out of college a second time.

Our college basketball team did well in 1988, finishing in second place at the national championships behind the Timberwolves from Minnesota. We set our collective sights on beating them in 1989. I also had my personal sights set on qualifying for the Olympic team that was going to Seoul, South Korea. I wanted to compete in the 800-meter women's wheelchair exhibition race.

At each Olympic Games, the International Olympic Committee tries out a few new sports. These are called exhibition sports, and if one is received favorably, it is upgraded to a demonstration sport. From there it can become a full-fledged Olympic sport with official records and medals. The Seoul games would be the second Olympics in which the 800-meter women's and the 1,500-meter men's wheelchair events would be exhibition sports.

I was awed at the idea of going to the Olympics, and I assumed my wins at the national games in 1987 would secure my place on the exhibition 800-meter team. I was sadly disappointed. I finished two places behind the qualifiers, though I still had a chance to compete on the Paralympic team. The Paralympic Games were

**I was determined not to flunk
out of college a second time.**

established in 1960 and are held in the same venues within two or three weeks of the Olympic Games. At the Paralympics, wheelchair athletes, dwarfs, amputees, athletes with cerebral palsy, and those with visual impairments compete in most of the same events contested in the Olympic Games, each competing within his or her own disability group.

Marty stressed that if I were going to have a chance at winning any medals at the Paralympics, I would have to do lots of sprint work. He soon had me doing basic weight training and intervals on the track. As I grew stronger, he increased the intensity of the workouts. By the time I got to Seoul, I was in the best shape I had ever been in.

While I was disappointed at not being in the exhibition event, the competitive spirit soon rose within me. I determined to win my events at the Paralympic Games. In the end, I came home with a gold medal in the 4x200 meter relay, a silver in the 4x100 meter relay, and two bronze medals for the 200- and 400-meter races. I was happy to win the medals, though I thought I could have done better. I didn't really comprehend the elite level of the athletes I had been up against.

When I got back to Illinois, I knew I had a lot of work ahead of me if I wanted to make the exhibition team going to the Olympic Games in Barcelona in 1992. A couple of weeks after I returned from Seoul, Marty Morse also revisited the issue of my trying a longer race.

I had just finished an hour on the roller when he came up to me. "To be honest with you, Jean, I'd like to see you do a marathon," he said. "You have good upper body strength, and I think you have what it takes to do well at it, especially if we can improve your endurance."

"But, Marty," I protested, "I don't want to do a marathon! It's way too long for me and I'm not interested." I thought people who wanted to race 26.2 miles were crazy. "I want to stick to the sprints."

"Okay," he said, "but I want you to think about it. It could be the challenge you need."

Challenge! I wanted to explode. Didn't Marty think that keeping my grades up, being on the women's basketball team, and training for racing were challenge enough for me?

Marty dropped the topic that day, but he kept bringing it up in the weeks to come. I began to feel that the only way to get him off my back was to agree to do a longer race—not a marathon, which was definitely out of my league, but maybe a 12-kilometer race.

When I told Marty I was willing to do a longer race, he put me right to work. I started doing more on-road training and building up my bench-pressing limit. I had felt pretty good about bench-pressing 160 pounds but knew my potential for getting stronger was great. Besides, it would help me in shorter races, too.

I had no illusions that I could beat someone as strong as Candace.

I had already competed twice in the Bloomsday, a 12-kilometer (7.46-mile) race held each May in Spokane, Washington. As I finished my sophomore final exams, I also trained for the race. I noticed that whenever my teammate Ann, Marty, and I talked about strategy for the race, one name would always come up—Candace Cable.

The names Candace Cable and Bloomsday were practically synonymous. Candace held the 12-kilometer record, and she had won every Bloomsday race from 1984 to 1988. The newspaper headlines said it all: "Can Candace Be Beaten?" and "The Woman Who Will Not Lose." I had met Candace Cable before and I knew of her reputation. She was thirty-two years old, from California, and she was the best female hill-climber in the world. Since Bloomsday was a very hilly course, she won by a long stretch every time.

I had no illusions that I could beat someone as strong as Candace. I just hoped I wouldn't make too big a fool out of myself during the race.

The day of the race was cold but sunny. Candace looked as confident as anyone I had ever seen. She smiled and greeted everyone with the poise of someone who had the race in the bag.

After the start, Candace set a fast pace for the race. However, I leaned forward and forced my wheels round until the muscles in my arms ached. After falling behind Candace on Doomsday Hill at mile five, I caught up to her again with a half-mile left to go in the race. As we approached the finish, it seemed that every muscle in my body was screaming in pain. Still, somewhere inside I found a reserve of energy. I began punching the wheels of my chair with my gloves more furiously than I had ever done. As I sprinted along, somehow I managed to pass Candace. I crossed the finish line three seconds ahead of her. I could hardly believe it. I had beaten Candace Cable! A surge of exhilaration and contentment coursed through me.

"Great job, Jean!" Marty yelled into the phone. "I'm so excited for you!"

Upon my return to Champaign, my teammates and friends congratulated me throughout the next day. Marty also congratulated me again, then suggested, "You know, Jean, the next step is a marathon. How about the Chicago Marathon?"

I stared at him. "But, Marty, I told you I don't want to do a marathon."

"Oh, you're in great shape already. Just do one and I'll never bother you again."

I didn't know what to say. Marty was, after all, my coach and I was supposed to take his advice seriously. Finally, I spoke. "Okay, I'll do the Chicago Marathon. But that's the *only* marathon I'll ever do."

Training with coach Marty Morse.

My welcome home after the Boston Marathon.

TEN

THE MOST SURREAL
MOMENT OF MY LIFE

"Go, Illinois. Go!" I could hear someone in the crowd yelling in response to my blue-and-white jersey. I made the 180-degree turn around the orange cones and headed back down the right side of the blocked off, four-lane highway on the last leg of the Chicago Marathon. The wind was behind me now. As I raced past athletes pushing the other way down the street (in this course we doubled back to complete the race), I got a good look at where the other women were. No one was anywhere close to me, and the only woman in front of me was my teammate, Ann Cody, with whom I had managed to stick until the mile twenty marker.

I was shocked to think I might be headed for second place! I'd had so many nightmares about never being able to finish such an impossibly long race. Even in my training I'd never actually gone 26.2 miles all at once. And going the distance wasn't my only fear. I was worried about getting lost on the course and ending up in some out-of-the-way Chicago side street. I also worried about dogs. Anyone who uses wheels (whether a bike, a car, or a chair) has at least one story about being chased by a dog. I had managed to avoid being bitten thus far into my career, but I'd had some close calls.

Finally I lifted my head and saw Grant Park directly in front of me. The finish line! Every muscle in my body ached, but I summoned my reserves for one final burst of speed. As I raced across the finish line in the park, my Cateye computer clocked in at 1 hour, 59 minutes, and 52 seconds. Eight seconds under two hours! I could hardly believe it. I had exceeded my highest expectations.

When I came out of the chute at the finish line, Marty rushed up to me with a bottle of water. As I gulped it down, he quizzed me. "Jean, do you realize what you just did?"

I nodded and wiped my mouth. "Yeah. I finished a marathon!" I exalted, grateful that none of the potential disasters had happened to me. I hadn't gotten lost on the course, nor had I been bitten by a dog. Most of all, I'd had the stamina to go the whole 26.2 miles.

"You did better than that, Jean!" he beamed, "You qualified for the Boston Marathon!"

His statement caught me off guard. I was ready to celebrate and relax, not think about another marathon. Naive as I was, it had never occurred to me that Marty would push me toward another marathon. Did he think I was a masochist?

"Marty, I told you I'd do one marathon and that's it. I don't want to do any more!"

Now it was Marty's turn to look incredulous. "But, Jean, you can't qualify for something as big as the Boston Marathon and not do it!"

"Well, I don't know," I said in a guarded tone. "My hands are blistered, my body hurts, and I don't know how long it will take me to recover. And what about my basketball season?"

For the time being we dropped the subject. I hoped it would be the last time he brought up the idea of my participating in another marathon. It was not. Over the coming weeks Marty worked on me relentlessly. He couldn't believe that I wouldn't accept the honor of competing in the most prestigious marathon in the world. In the end, I gave in and told him I would try the Boston Marathon. Again I told him I'd do it once—and only once.

In January 1990, Ann Cody and I began to focus on Boston as well as on the basketball championships. Instead of doing fifty miles of roadwork a week, we pushed our way around a hundred miles of Champaign countryside and did time trials into a headwind.

The Boston course is known for its hills, and the flat prairie landscape is a far from ideal place to train for hills. One of the best alternatives we came up with were the ramps around the University of Illinois Assembly Hall, where the school's basketball teams practiced and played. In our everyday wheelchairs we took turns towing each other up the long ramps, then racing down again. Initially this was very straining, but after a while it became easier. Much to my dismay, however, Marty came up with another towing exercise. On the flat he would repeatedly add another person to the line to be towed until Ann and I were taking turns pulling five other wheelchair athletes behind us. When I tried pulling six people behind me, I couldn't get the traction I needed to move. My wheels just spun in place. It was no wonder. When I added it up,

I had over seven hundred pounds hanging off the back of my chair!

All in all, I practiced harder than I had ever done before, and in March I went to the Los Angeles Marathon to test my fitness. I hoped to come in near the front of the pack as I had in Chicago.

I was nervous about the race for a number of reasons, the most important being that I was not using my own racing chair. Because I wasn't as tall as most of the other athletes, Marty thought I might be better off using a chair with twenty-six-inch wheels instead of the usual twenty-seven-inch ones. My own yellow racing frame wasn't built to accommodate wheels that size, so Marty suggested I try one of my teammate's chairs that had twenty-six-inch wheels.

The new chair had another difference, too. The threads on the axle were a half-inch wide, while the ones on my chair were a quarter-inch. I didn't own an Allen wrench that large, but I was certain Ann did. So, being a poor student, I decided not to spend my money on one for myself. I would just borrow Ann's.

Alas, when we got to our hotel room and started unpacking our frames from their travel boxes and putting them together, we discovered Ann had left her large wrench back in Champaign. I was panicked. The thing I hated most was not being fully prepared, and this time I wasn't. I hoped it wasn't an omen of things to come.

Ann and I did the best we could with what was available. I took a hotel washcloth and wrapped it around the wrench I did have until I had made it large enough to fit into the sockets of the wheels. After a few turns, the wheels seemed to be attached securely enough to the frame. I hoped it would hold together for the race.

The day of the race was gray and overcast, and the crowd was thin. Instead of being in my own "lucky" yellow wheelchair, I was in the borrowed blue chair with the rigged axle. I felt understandably nervous. Still, the adrenaline started pumping in me as the starter's gun fired. Ann and I led the field until she dropped me at mile seven. As I passed mile nine, I looked down at the wheel. My heart skipped a beat. The wheel was working its way out of the axle sleeve, rubbing against the frame as it did so. Panic-stricken, I surveyed my surroundings. There, in front of me was the answer to my prayers: a gas station and garage.

I rolled into the gas station. "Could somebody please help me?" I yelled. "I need a half-inch Allen wrench."

A man in greasy overalls strolled out of the shop. As I repeated my plea, he stared back at me blankly.

A second, younger man joined him. "Español," he said. "Yo hablo Español."

I couldn't believe it. These were Spanish-speaking mechanics. The only Spanish I knew came from watching *Sesame Street* while I had been a nanny. My heart sank.

"Does anyone speak English?" I yelled, looking desperately at a third man filling a gallon container with gas. He shrugged his shoulders at me.

I looked back at the course as four male athletes whooshed by. I knew there had to be a half-inch Allen wrench in the garage somewhere. I just had to figure out how to communicate with these men.

I rolled inside to the work area, and there lying on a bench was a monster Allen wrench. I pointed at the wrench, then at the axle and back again. Still more blank stares. I repeated the action, speaking slowly in English this time. No luck.

I glanced out the door. The women I had managed to leave far behind were now all streaming past in a pack. I was so frustrated I could scream. I tried again. Still no recognition. Ten valuable minutes ticked by before I was able to get anyone to understand that I

Fifteen minutes after I had stopped, the wheel was finally secure again.

---

needed a *tiny* Allen wrench. One of the attendants rummaged around in a wooden box and found the right one. However, he wouldn't give it to me. He insisted on screwing the wheel back on for me, very slowly. I was frantic by now, watching the back of the pack straggle past me. I reached out and grabbed the wrench from his hand, but he took it back firmly and continued at his own pace. I felt my blood pressure rising to the point where I wanted to explode. Fifteen minutes after I had stopped, the wheel was finally secure again, and I rolled out of the garage and back onto the course.

Half a mile later I felt the first splatters of rain. "Where did this come from?" I asked myself. There had been no mention of it on the weather forecast and, just like with the Allen wrench, I was not prepared for it. Wheelchair athletes use a sticky substance called klister to stop their hands from slipping on the pushrims in the rain. We squeeze the klister out of a tube and onto our gloves and/or the pushrims. The klister is slightly sticky, and the wetter it gets the stickier it becomes. Professional skiers use it on wet snow. It's great stuff if you have it. I did not. My tube was safely in my tool bag back in the hotel room.

The rain began to come down heavily, soaking my Lycra outfit and waterlogging my leather gloves. They became unmanageable but there was no way to squeeze the water out. The gloves were taped securely onto my hands. It was a disaster. Once again I chastised myself for letting Marty talk me into doing another ridiculous marathon.

All in all, it took me two hours and thirty-five minutes to make it to the finish line. When I got back to the hotel room Ann was waiting anxiously for me. "What happened to you?" she asked, "Did you crash? Did you get lost?"

I told her the long, sorry story about the Allen wrench and the klister.

"Whoa," she said. "You had a bad day."

"Man, did I ever!" I replied. "I promised Marty I'd do the Boston Marathon, but that's going to be the last marathon I do. Ever! It's crazy racing that far. I'm going to stick to the shorter distances."

Thankfully, the Women's Wheelchair Basketball National Championships were looming, and I had little time to dwell on the upcoming Boston Marathon. Our team was in great shape, and we wanted desperately to beat the Minnesota Timberwolves, whom we had narrowly lost to in the last two national championship games.

Each game we played in the championship competition was hotly contested, but somehow the University of Illinois team managed to prevail and win each one. And then we won the championship game! The national title was ours. The whole team was elated, but as much as I wanted to stay "in the moment," I knew I had final exams and the Boston Marathon to complete in the month ahead.

In the brief interval between winning the national basketball title and competing in the Boston Marathon, Ann and I worked out together in Champaign. It was discouraging comparing myself to Ann. She was so much stronger than me and more practiced. Whenever we went for a twenty-mile push, she would finish several minutes ahead of me, and on the rollers she averaged a mile an hour faster than I did. By the time we boarded the airplane for the flight to Boston, I knew I shouldn't be going at all. Certainly Ann should be representing the university; I didn't belong in such a grueling race.

Sleep wouldn't come to me on Saturday night, two nights before the start of the marathon. I tossed and turned, nervously thinking about the distance and the fabled hills. The following morning I wished I had the courage to tell Marty I was going to pull out, but I didn't. Instead I got in a van with him and several of the other wheelchair athletes from Champaign and we drove the course.

Paul, our driver, weaved his way to the start of the race in Hopkinton, twenty-six miles west of Boston. Once we were on the course, my eyes were glued to the terrain. The course started out on a downhill slope. The first six miles were mostly downhill, despite some short climbs. It then flattened out for a while. I began to relax; it didn't look too intimidating after all.

At the mile eight marker, the course began a series of gentle climbs punctuated by a number of flat stretches. These lasted until we made a right turn at the Newton firehouse. I took a deep breath; the course had just become a whole lot more challenging. The hill we were driving up was steep! At mile nineteen, the van slowed down so we could closely study the terrain.

"This is the beginning of Heartbreak Hill," said Marty.

I nodded. So this was the infamous Heartbreak Hill. It looked every bit as intimidating as its reputation. I thought about my hill training. The only hills with names in Champaign were the man-made overpasses crossing three interstates. I wondered how I would cope with such a long hill so late in the course—or rather, several hills, as Heartbreak Hill is actually a series of back-to-back inclines over a two-mile stretch of road. The longer we climbed, the steeper it got. The drive down the other side was just as steep, which concerned me too. It would be easy to lose control of one's chair and go careening down a hill. I tried not to imagine myself crashing at the bottom.

Marty broke into my thoughts. "Jean," he said. "I've talked with Ann and this is how I want you to work it."

I kept watching out the window as the van drove down Commonwealth Avenue. "Okay," I replied.

"We need someone from Illinois to take this race from Connie Hansen. You know it's hers to lose. You'll have to watch Candace Cable, too. She's going to be wanting the title back."

That's for sure! I thought to myself, going over her record in my mind. Since the women's wheelchair division had been introduced in 1977, Candace Cable had won the race six out of thirteen times, including 1985, 1986, 1987, and 1988. Last year had been a phenomenally fast race. Connie Hansen from Denmark had beaten Candace's world record by more than eight minutes in a stunning 1 hour, 50 minutes, and 6 seconds. Candace had broken the two-hour barrier as well, but she was 2 minutes and 28 seconds behind Connie.

"You're job is to back up Ann," Marty went on. "Stick with her as long as you can and when she's ready to make a break for it, take a pull and slow the pack down."

"I can do that," I said. We'd gone over this before. Wheelchair racing is much like professional cycling, and team members often work together to help one of them win. A teammate will sacrifice her own chances to keep the pack back from her teammate. However, in this case, if I were able to help Ann, I wouldn't be sacrificing my chances. There was no way I could beat Candace Cable or Connie Hansen.

"Thanks," said Ann. "Tell you what. If you think you can help me get away, say the number '15' and I'll make a break for it."

"Okay," I said as the van drove on past the finish line. *Let Ann be the first one across the line,* I prayed silently.

That night I didn't sleep well, either. I now had the imprint of the course on my mind to keep me awake.

The next morning, Monday, April 16, 1990, it seemed as if the whole of Boston was caught up in the impending marathon.

Everywhere I looked there were blue-and-white banners and balloons with the marathon logo, the head of a silver unicorn. As I pushed the half-mile from my hotel to the Sheraton Hotel, I tried to keep calm. But it was stressful to realize I was about to race in the world's oldest and most prestigious road race. I just hoped I could do it.

Ann and I boarded one of the many buses waiting at the Sheraton to take the racers west of Boston to Hopkinton. I was glad we had driven the course the day before, though I still felt unprepared.

There had been a chain-reaction crash at the start of the race three years before.

It was nearly four hours from the time we left the hotel until the time the race was due to start. The wheelchair division was scheduled to begin fifteen minutes before the runners, and I was nervous about the start. There had been a chain-reaction crash at the start of the race three years before in 1987, and the rules had been changed so that a pace vehicle now controlled the downhill start of the race for the first half-mile. It drove at a steady fourteen miles an hour. Although it had made the beginning safer, Ann warned me that it had not eliminated the possibility of crashing since so many wheelchairs were jammed close together. If ever there was a time for defensive driving, this was it. The paced start also added another complication. If an athlete passed the pace car or left the lane, he or she was automatically disqualified. I told myself to be extra careful. I didn't want that to happen to me.

I began preparing myself for the start of the race. Firmly, I

strapped myself into my racing chair and then put on my aerodynamic helmet. Next I slid on my leather gloves, pulling their Velcro bands tight around my wrists. Finally, I gave my chair a final
check. Everything seemed in order.

The pace car revved up and we were off. I was two places over
from Ann, and I kept watch for her out of the corner of my eye.
Her win was a win for Marty and for the University of Illinois, and
I reminded myself that was all that mattered.

The first half-mile passed without incident, and the pace car
drove off, leaving the women in the field to sort themselves out. By
now a rule had been made that men and women could not draft
off each other. The races were considered separate events, and any
interference from an athlete in the other event would mean immediate disqualification. This meant we had to be very diligent to
keep out of each other's drafts. Women could pull up beside a man,
but not behind him.

We stayed in a bunch to begin with, but by mile eight a front
pack, consisting of Ann, Connie, and me, had formed. I remained
determined to stay with Ann as long as I could. Everything went
well. Unlike some races, each of us followed racing protocol and
took our turn out in front taking a pull, then fell back in behind
the new leader.

We had a tailwind, which helped a lot. By this time Connie
was in front, Ann was second, and I was third. I checked my Cateye computer; we were clipping along at fifteen miles per hour.

"Time to pull," Connie yelled, slowing down so she could fall
to the back of the pack while Ann took her place at the front. This
left me in the middle. As Connie Hansen dropped back behind me

I could see she was tired. Ann set a strong pace at the head of the pack, and immediately I turned my head and looked back. Connie appeared to be struggling to keep up, and her head was tucked way down.

"Fifteen," I said in a quiet voice, hoping Ann would hear me. She must have, because she surged forward and I slowed the pace down to fourteen miles per hour to let her get away. By the time Connie Hansen looked up and noticed what we had done, Ann had opened up a seventy-five-meter gap on us.

I continued to pull, confident I had given my teammate the opportunity she needed. I started to climb the first of many steep hills in Newton. I was amazed that I was still with the front runners, and I began to think that I might be able to beat Connie and get second place! However, by the time I was halfway up the hill I was very frustrated. I had yelled for Connie to take a turn pulling twice, but she hadn't come up to the front. *Why is she doing this?* I asked myself. *She knows the protocol, and it's her turn.*

I turned my head and looked back to say something to her, but she wasn't in my draft as I had assumed. She was a good thirty meters behind me. I could hardly believe my eyes. Suddenly it hit me. If I could keep this gap between us, I could indeed come in second place. Going down the hill, though, Connie began to gain on me. She was obviously a stronger downhill athlete than I was. Still, I maintained the lead over her at the bottom as we headed for the infamous two-mile-long Heartbreak Hill. As we started on the hill, I forced my arms to push harder and harder. Once again the gap between Connie and me widened. By mile nineteen I had left Connie behind and was catching up to Ann. She seemed to slow down, as if she were waiting for me. I caught her at mile twenty and went up to the front when she asked me to pull. We usually traded places pulling at the front every minute while training back in Champaign, and I knew I was strong enough to take my turn now.

I did my minute and waited for Ann to take her turn. She didn't come up and pass me right away, and I began to get a little frustrated with her. I thought the whole thing was a little unfair. First I had stalled Connie so she could get away, and then I had lost Connie myself and pushed really hard to catch up with Ann so I could let her rest for a minute. Now I needed a break. It was her turn to pull!

I turned around to tell her I needed help and was stunned by what I saw. Ann had dropped back thirty meters behind me. I tried to process this information but my mind was numb. Goosebumps ran up my neck. I was in the lead at the Boston Marathon! And not just as a tactic to get my teammate into position. No, I was in the lead for real. I hardly knew what to do. I had never rehearsed this possibility. Adrenaline surged through me as I realized I might win the race. I pushed forward, widening the gap between Ann and me to fifty meters.

I crested Heartbreak Hill well in front of the other women and determined to give winning the race my best shot. As I started down the other side of the hill I glanced at my Cateye computer. I noted its readout and quickly did the math in my head twice to make sure I hadn't made a mistake. I knew Connie Hansen had set the world record at 1:50:06, and here I was at mile twenty-three in just under ninety minutes. If I kept up this pace I would break her record!

My emotions went wild, and I pumped my arms with all my might. I had just over three miles to go. Could I do it? I tried to discipline myself not to look back because I knew that I slowed down every time I turned my head.

Instead, I relied on my Cateye to keep me motivated. I was stunned at the pace I was keeping. I turned onto Boylston Street and saw the large banner that read "Finish." I was nearly there! I didn't let up one bit until I surged across the finish line.

"And Jean Driscoll from Illinois comes in at 1:43:17, beating the world record by almost seven minutes!" I heard the PA announcer say.

I could hardly believe it. It was like they were talking about someone else. Ann came in one minute and eight seconds behind me, and Connie Hansen was twenty-three seconds behind her. I sat there in a daze while an official placed a laurel wreath on my head. "The Star-Spangled Banner" began to play, not for any other athlete, but for me, Jean Driscoll. It was the most surreal moment of my life.

At Peachtree 10K in Atlanta with Louise Sauvage drafting behind me.

Debbie Richardson helped in many ways, including celebrating in 1992.

ELEVEN

ALL THE PIECES
FITTED TOGETHER

Winning the Boston Marathon changed my life forever. The media's lens focused on me as never before. Camera crews came out to the university to interview me; I appeared on sports and general-interest TV shows. This all came as quite a shock, especially since I had given absolutely no thought at all to winning. I had booked a flight out of Boston several hours after the finish of the marathon, never for a moment thinking I would need to stay for the awards ceremony. I hastily rescheduled my flight so I could accept the silver trophy in person.

The win was wonderful on a financial level too. I won a total of $25,000: $7,500 for finishing first, $7,500 for setting a new course record, and $10,000 for setting a new world record.

It took me no time at all to figure out what to do with the money. My old '78 Cutlass Supreme was slowly dying. For the last three years I hadn't been able to trust it on trips, so I'd taken a Greyhound bus or rented a car when I wanted to visit my family and friends in Milwaukee. I did my homework, investigating my options. Finally, I decided on a midnight blue 1990 Dodge Caravan. It was such a great feeling to lay down cash for the whole purchase price. I could hardly comprehend that the vehicle was mine. When I got back to the apartment I kept peeking out the window to make sure I wasn't dreaming. In addition to the car, the money allowed me to pay off my racing expenses and catch up on bills.

However, there's nothing like final exams to bring a person down to earth in a hurry, and I had to study hard so I could complete my junior year at the University of Illinois. I was already booked to attend several more athletic events, one of which was the Goodwill Games in Seattle in July. Ann and I were the two main contenders in the 1,500-meter race. When the day arrived, I beat her by one one-hundredth of a second, breaking the world record and winning the gold medal. A photo of this event was featured on a Hallmark card.

In January 1991, I completed my bachelor's degree in speech communication with honors. Other members of my family were meeting their goals too. Francie earned a B.S. in political science that year, and Ron an A.A. in electronics. Mom threw us all a triple graduation party. I was ready to celebrate. Getting my B.A. meant just as much to me as winning the Boston Marathon. I was finally able to lay to rest the ghost of flunking out. I also knew I would need a solid credential behind me when my racing career ended, so I enrolled in the master's program for rehabilitation administration at the University of Illinois. This degree would allow me to run a rehabilitation facility: the type of center with which I was very familiar.

I continued with the athletics program and also began volunteering as an assistant coach. Even after my Boston win, I still preferred the 800-meter and 1,500-meter events, but I was no longer set against the idea of doing another marathon. I also started training for another year of basketball. We had the national title to defend against the notorious Timberwolves.

As the next year came around, I began to train seriously for my second Boston Marathon. However, I didn't expect to win, mainly because Ann Cody beat me in just about every practice session we had. I figured I'd had my moment of glory and it was Ann's turn.

Much to my surprise, I broke away from Ann and Connie Hansen at the seventeen-mile mark and never saw them again. I bettered the previous year's time, winning in 1:42:42, thirty-five seconds faster than before.

During the summer of 1991, I broke the national and world records in the 800-meter and 1,500-meter track events, and in the 10-kilometer Peachtree Road Race in Atlanta. I was flying high, breaking a record a month!

In July, I also heard that I had been nominated for the Women's Sports Foundation's Sudafed Amateur Sportswoman of the Year Award. Once again, I was clueless as to what a huge honor it was to be nominated. I had no idea that famous athletes like Jackie Joyner-Kersee and Bonnie Blair had won it in the past.

I was thrilled to make it to the top ten. When I read the names of some of the other nominees, including Lyn Jennings and Kristi Yamaguchi, I knew I would never win the award. Elite wheelchair athletes were not typically respected as world-class athletes in the sports world. Every once in a while we were given a cursory nod, but seldom a serious consideration alongside able-bodied athletes. I thought it was nice of them to include me on their top-ten list.

One Tuesday morning in September as I was getting ready to do a road workout, the phone rang.

"Hello, Jean, this is Jenifer Miller from the Women's Sports Foundation. I'm calling to let you know that the votes are in for the Sportswoman of the Year, and you won!"

I nearly dropped the phone. I was too flabbergasted to speak. The members of the foundation had voted for me! I couldn't believe it.

"What do you think?" Jenifer asked me. "Are you excited?"

"Yes," I stammered, feeling completely flabbergasted. I couldn't wait to get off the phone to tell Marty, Ann, and my roommate, Amy.

"I'm sending you an information packet overnight. The event will be held in New York City on Monday, October 7. You need to be there on Sunday afternoon. There's a breakfast Monday morning and, of course, the awards dinner is that evening. It's a black-tie event. We'll pay your expenses and take good care of you."

"Thank you," I said weakly.

"It's always a lot of fun, especially the dinner. You'll meet a lot of people. Call me when you've read the packet and we'll iron out the details."

"Okay," I responded in amazement, "Thank you so much! Please thank everyone on the awards committee!"

After Jenifer hung up, I sat for a long time trying to take in what she had just told me. I, Jean Driscoll from Milwaukee, was the 1991 Amateur Sportswoman of the Year. In the end I burst out laughing, it was so unbelievable. I couldn't wait to tell everyone I knew.

Fortunately, I had a wonderful roommate, Amy Gregson, who helped me get ready for the event. Together we began making a list of all the things I would need to buy. At the top of the list was a suitable dress. Just about everything I wore came from Target or other discount clothing stores, and now I needed to upgrade to something more lavish. I had never attended a black-tie dinner before. All my information about such events came via television specials such as the Academy Awards and shows like *Entertainment Tonight,* which I watched occasionally.

I knew it was going to be my night to shine!

**In the end I burst out laughing,
it was so unbelievable.**

Amy went shopping with me one day in Champaign, and I tried on all sorts of dresses. Eventually, though, I found the dress of my dreams in Chicago. It was a glamorous royal blue sheath, adorned all over with sequins and beads. It made me feel like a movie star. Normally, I wouldn't dream of paying $550 for a dress, but this was a very special occasion. I used some of my Boston Marathon winnings to pay for it. Of course, a dress doesn't constitute a whole outfit, so I also had to find the perfect pair of glittery blue shoes, a handbag, and a white lace shawl to match.

For most of the time as I prepared for my trip to New York I was in a state of shock, and I was glad when Amy offered to accompany me. She helped allay my fears that I wouldn't know anyone and would be alone in a strange place.

We flew into the Big Apple on Sunday morning and were met

by Tuti and Sadie, two interns from the Women's Sports Foundation. They whisked us away in a big black Lincoln Towncar to the Marriott Marquis Hotel, in the heart of Manhattan. From the time I arrived until I left, nearly every minute was accounted for. Tuti and Sadie made sure I found my way to where I needed to be. And I was treated like a queen.

The festivities began Sunday night with a VIP social at a sports bar. The next morning there was an athletes' breakfast, where more than one hundred of the nation's top female athletes had an opportunity to mix and mingle. There were field and ice hockey players, top-seeded tennis players, runners, soccer players, and swimmers, among others.

After breakfast it was time for everyone except the award winners to practice the grand march. I wasn't in this, so I was taken to do some phone interviews. Then we all had lunch together, followed by hair and makeup appointments courtesy of the Women's Sports Foundation. They had arranged for Jacob Neil and Associates to set up shop in a couple of ornate meeting rooms at the hotel. My first stop was the hairdresser. We were told to arrive with our hair washed and wet; the hairdresser took it from there. My hair was blow-dried and swirled on top of my head in a French twist. While this was being done I joked with Tracy Austin, the tennis player, who was having her makeup done. Then it was on to the next stop.

I sat still while I was pampered with my first professional cosmetics job. A little later a manicurist was filing and painting my fingernails. I felt as if I was living a page straight out of *People* magazine. When it was all over I looked at myself in the mirror. It was an astonishing transformation. I couldn't help but stare in the mirror at the Midwestern girl with the Manhattan makeover. I was ready for my first glamour party.

Amy helped me carefully zip up my dress so I didn't disrupt my makeup, nails, or hair. For the first time in my life I felt truly elegant, and I hoped lots of pictures would be taken. I need not have worried. When we got downstairs, the ballroom was swarming with the media. The athletes, the media, and the dinner sponsors all mingled together during the cocktail hour. Amy was there, as well, capturing the evening on film.

I tried to remember the people who talked to me, but there were so many. There was Lyn St. James, the racecar driver, and Jackie Tonawanda, a boxer whose business card billed her as the "Female Ali." As well as the athletes themselves, all kinds of other people connected with sports were there. Big corporations like Clairol, Ocean Spray, and Sara Lee were represented, along with officials from the NBA, the LPGA, and many other sports bodies. *Entertainment Tonight* was there, and even their cameramen were wearing tuxedos.

After an hour, Tuti and Sadie, who stuck with me like klister, showed me to a table at the front of the room. The table was sponsored by ESPN, and sportscaster Robin Roberts stood up to welcome me. It was all a little mind-boggling. Soon the orchestra on stage began to play, and Diana Nyad, the first woman to swim the English Channel, moved to the microphone to begin the grand march of athletes. One by one, each of the top athletes from the various sports was introduced and a few of their career highlights were mentioned.

When the march was finished, we ate dinner and I joined in conversation with the people from ESPN who were seated at the table. Toward the end of the meal the awards program began. I sat through most of it before Tuti and Sadie escorted me to the backstage area. The stage was not wheelchair accessible, so two assistants hoisted me up eight steps onto it. I sat behind the curtain at the back of the stage while a two-minute video clip featuring my achievements was played.

"And now, I want you all to join me in welcoming the 1991 Amateur Sportswoman of the Year, Miss Jean Driscoll."

I rolled out onto the stage and blinked. Powerful lights shone in my eyes, but I knew where I was headed. None other than Jackie Joyner-Kersee was waiting to present the award to me.

The crowd gave me a standing ovation, which I had been told was customary when the winner was introduced. Jackie handed me the microphone and I waited for the applause to die down before I spoke.

During my brief acceptance speech I talked about how wheelchair sports were growing and developing in a manner parallel to women's sports. Not long ago society had considered women too fragile and delicate to be serious competitors, but now women were excelling in every sport. Wheelchair sports were on the same path. Until very recently a person in a wheelchair was referred to as a victim or an invalid, but now the sports community was making way for us and we were beginning to shine.

When I finished, the audience members sprang to their feet again, clapping loudly. At the time I thought this was normal too. But afterward, people from the Women's Sports Foundation and other athletes told me that this did not always happen.

After receiving the Amateur Sportswoman of the Year award,

my fame seemed to increase exponentially. The mayor of Champaign and the mayor of neighboring Urbana got together and proclaimed February 7, 1992, "Jean Driscoll Day." It coincided with a University of Illinois able-bodied women's basketball home game. The coach wanted to honor me at halftime. It was a great feeling to have a day named after me.

I also got to sing the national anthem for the first time publicly at that game, a goal of mine when I had seen another athlete do it. Music had always been important in our family, and I enjoyed singing and writing music of my own. On my day, I was presented with a variety of gifts from the two mayors, the chancellor of the university, the dean of my graduate college, and the head women's coach. The bouquets of flowers kept coming and coming.

Another wonderful thing happened in the aftermath of Jean Driscoll Day, something that would profoundly change my life. The person primarily responsible for putting the day together was Debbie Richardson. I was introduced to her on January 17 and was instantly impressed with her. I couldn't remember meeting anyone as positive as she was. Her eyes and smile radiated an inner peace that had eluded me all of my life.

After Jean Driscoll Day was over, I continued to get to know Debbie better. About six weeks later she invited me to her house to meet some friends she had told me about who were visiting from Georgia. From then on, we often went out for lunch or watched a movie together.

As I talked with Debbie, I found she had a deep faith in God that seemed to carry her through some of life's most difficult challenges. I contrasted her peace and acceptance with my own deeply rooted bitterness and anger about many of my experiences. Growing older, getting a degree, winning two marathons and many other races and titles had helped me to bury much of the pain I felt about my childhood. But I knew it was still there, swept under the surface of a busy life. Debbie invited me to go to church with her three separate times, but I was still leery about getting involved in anything to do with religion. Finally I decided to give it a try as long as Debbie stayed close beside me. I had no intention of being a sitting target for any religious zealot who wanted to pray for my healing or confront me about my lack of faith, as people had done in the past.

Debbie's relationship with Jesus was completely different from my impression of what knowing God was like.

One Sunday morning in late April, Debbie drove me to Windsor Road Christian Church. It wasn't as bad as I thought it would be, but I felt pretty uncomfortable anyway. Still, after that I would go with her to church if I happened to be in Champaign for the weekend, which was only about half the time because of my sports schedule. I kept thinking about the things Debbie said in response to my questions about God and the Bible. The most startling thing was that Debbie's relationship with Jesus was completely different from my impression of what knowing God was like.

The more I got to know Debbie the more impressed I was with

her Christian experience. Unlike the faith-healing meetings I had been dragged to as a teenager, there was nothing phony about her religion. I could see that it came from her heart, sustaining her spirit and giving her a peace that had always eluded me. I found the same peace and joy in many of Debbie's church friends, and it was something I wanted in my own life.

I knew that at the O'Briens' house I had asked Jesus into my heart. But even though I was going to church at the time, I knew little about what I was doing, and my new commitment hadn't influenced my everyday life at all. I was like the seed that fell on the rock. Once I left the O'Briens' home, I stopped even thinking about Jesus.

At about the same time as my relationship with Debbie was growing, I became extremely busy again. I sang the national anthem at the 1992 Milwaukee Brewer's home opener. I won another Boston Marathon, shaving nearly six minutes off the record I'd set the year before. Yet despite my busy schedule of graduate school, racing, and volunteer coaching, I still wanted to explore the issue of faith. By May, I was reading the Bible and thinking a lot about the meaning and direction of my life.

I continued to talk with Debbie, asking her questions and weighing her answers. Now, after talking to Debbie, I could see there was a lot more to being a Christian than saying just one simple prayer. It was a way of viewing and responding to every situation. Finally, in late June, I came to the point where I knew God was real and that I needed him active in my life. Once again in the privacy of my bedroom I prayed. This time committing my *entire* life to Christ.

The joy that flooded into my life after that moment was a

hundred times greater than the thrill of winning the Boston Marathon. It's hard to explain to people, but for the first time in my life I felt as though all the pieces fitted together.

All this happened as I was training for the Women's Wheelchair 800-Meter Exhibition Event to be held at the Olympic Games in Barcelona, Spain. I reached an athletic peak during the qualifying trials and became the number-one qualifier for the event.

On July 20, 1992, I boarded a plane for Tampa, Florida, the processing site for the U.S. Olympic Team. While there we were given instructions on the various aspects of being an Olympian. We were told how the drug testing was done, given some tips on Spanish culture, and photographed in our official outfits. We were divided into groups according to our sports, and each individual was given a shopping cart. A paper with our name and event was handed to each of us, and on it was listed all the clothes we were to be issued as members of the Olympic Team. We were instructed to work our way around a huge room that had tables and boxes piled high with a variety of clothing items.

I pushed the cart with one hand and wheeled my chair with the other. My first stop was for three polo shirts. Then it was on to socks, track uniforms, hats, warmup outfits, T-shirts, athletic shoes, jackets, sunglasses, and more. Near the end of the line I was measured for everything from an Olympic ring to a black leather jacket, which I was told would be sent to my home after the Olympic Games were over. Each of us was also given a Cabbage Patch doll complete with a white Olympic T-shirt, red-white-and-blue warmup outfit and sneakers! All this was provided by Reebok, the official Olympic outfitter for that year.

Working together, we helped each other cram our new wardrobes into our new, extra-large suitcases. Then we were off to catch the charter flight to Spain. I was glad to sit down on the plane. Being in such a high profile event was exhausting, and I hadn't even arrived yet!

On the flight, a man who introduced himself as George asked to sit beside me. We chatted for a while. I told him about my train-ing, and he told me about his family and his freight business. About halfway through the conversation I noticed he was wearing an enormous ring. Having just been measured for a ring myself, I commented on it.

George took it off for me to have a closer look. It had "1978" engraved on one side and the New York Yankees' insignia on the other. It looked like an oversized class ring. "Oh," I said, thinking he was the vice commissioner of major league baseball. "Do you have one of those for each year?" I asked.

He laughed, "Only when we win. You don't know who I am, do you?"

I shook my head, "I know your face, but I can't place you right now."

He laughed again. "I'm George Steinbrenner, owner of the New York Yankees."

"Ohhh," I said, feeling very foolish. "And that's a real World Series ring?"

"Yes, it is," he smiled. "Now tell me when your event is. I want to come and watch you."

For the rest of the flight all I could think was, I can't believe I didn't recognize George Steinbrenner. Wait until Ray and Ron find out!

The wheelchair exhibition athletes didn't stay at the Olympic village, but I had to go there to the sports medicine facility each day for treatment on some strained muscles. Each time the icing and ultrasound sessions were done, I would roll down to the beautiful Mediterranean Sea. It was located just two blocks from the athletes' village. For the first time in my travels I had taken a Bible with me, and I would sit at the water's edge and read it quietly. The more I read and prayed, the more calm and centered my life became.

I didn't win the gold medal in Barcelona, but I did take second place behind Connie Hansen, my Danish rival in the Boston Marathon. The queen of Spain presented me with my silver medal. Naturally, I would have preferred to win the gold. But even though I didn't, I felt strangely content with the way my life was shaping up. I was now an Olympic medalist!

In January 1993, I completed my master's degree, erasing any doubt in my mind that I belonged in college. I was also very relieved. After five years of juggling athletics and academics, I was now free to concentrate on sports.

Marty Morse didn't want to lose athletes from the program at the University of Illinois if he could help it, so he created a new status for graduate students and alumni. He called it Professional Athletic Staff. This volunteer position enabled an athlete to continue to

ALL THE PIECES FITTED TOGETHER   **163**

train with him in exchange for part-time assistant coaching and other related work. When Marty spoke to me about the idea, I jumped at the chance. I wasn't done with racing yet, and I loved training in Champaign.

———

**When Marty spoke to me about the idea,
I jumped at the chance.**

———

That year in Boston, everyone seemed to be experimenting with new technology on their racing chairs, primarily making their wheels more aerodynamic. As I waited for the race to begin, I hoped that once again I could win and maybe set a new record. In my past three wins, Ann Cody and Connie Hansen had jostled for second and third place. But this year there was a new athlete in the pack, a nineteen-year-old from Australia named Louise Sauvage. Although I had never seen her in action, some of my friends told me she could tear up the track.

The race that year turned on tactics. I tried to break away from the others several times and finally succeeded at mile eleven. I led the pack the rest of the way, crossing the finish line in 1:34:50, breaking the world, course, and my personal records yet again. Newspaper headlines declared, "Jean Is Queen of the Hills" and "Driscoll Grabs Four-peat."

I was flattered, and I had to admit I had a handy lead. Connie Hansen came in at 1:35:42. And Louise Sauvage, the newcomer, was third in 1:39:31.

Following the win there was the familiar excitement of award ceremonies and press receptions. But there was something else as well. Newly elected President Bill Clinton invited the men's and women's winners in the open, masters, and wheelchair divisions to the White House. Once there we went on a three-mile run with the president—and what seemed like an army of Secret Service agents—around Haynes Point. Then we went back to the White House for a photo session in the Rose Garden.

Just like the Sportswoman of the Year Award ceremony the previous year, the whole experience was difficult to take in. It hardly seemed real at the time, though when I got home I had the pictures to prove I had really been there. The question became, would I join the Boston Marathon winners in the Rose Garden again next year?

Boston features a billboard-size screen for viewing the race.

The 1996 Paralympics with Louise Sauvage.

TWELVE

WINNING WAS IN MY BLOOD

As I drove the eighteen-hour trip to Boston in 1994, I had lots of time to think about my recent losses. Louise Sauvage, the young Australian athlete, was a much stronger competitor than I had given her credit for. Since Christmas she had beaten me in the Gasparilla 15-kilometer race in Tampa, Florida, and in the Mobil World Wheelchair Challenge Criterium in Torrance, California. I actually came in third in both races, with Connie Hansen coming second at Gasparilla and Tanni Grey from Wales beating me at Torrance. Neither of these races had any significant climbs, and I couldn't wait for Boston with its long, steep hills. *That's my course,* I told myself.

Driving through the Appalachian Mountains, I visualized myself pushing up every hill on the course as steadily and smoothly as my van was cruising up the windy mountain slopes. In my mind I worked though every possible scenario, developing different strategies to deal with various circumstances. However, there was one obstacle I didn't predict and it nearly forced me to abandon the race at the six-mile mark.

On the Friday night before the marathon, fourteen of us went out for dinner. There was my coach, Marty, and his wife, Karen; his brother and sister-in-law, Sam and Trish; some of his other relatives; members of the athletic staff from the University of Illinois; and several other athletes. Being in Boston, we decided to go to a seafood restaurant. The food was great and so was the company. I arrived back at the hotel late and went straight to bed.

I was awakened at 7 A.M. by the sound of the telephone. Blurry-eyed, I picked it up.

"Hi, Jean, it's Trish. How are you?" Trish's voice had an urgency to it that caught me off guard.

"I'm fine," I replied, "What's up?"

"Oh, thank goodness," she went on. "Marty's been throwing up half the night, and Karen and Eleanor are sick too."

"What is it?" I asked.

"It's got to be something we ate last night, possibly the clam chowder. Except you had that, too, didn't you?"

"Yes," I said. "But I feel fine."

"Well, that's the main thing," Trish said. "You're the one with the marathon to win on Monday."

"Tell Marty I hope he feels better soon," I said.

I hung up the phone and lay back in bed, thinking of everything I had to do that day. There was the prerace press conference and then the traditional pizza party at Trish and Sam's house in the late afternoon. That was always something to look forward to. Sam and Trish made the best pizzas from scratch, and there were so many friends and well-wishers there to get me pumped up. I loved going to the event.

Ten minutes later I decided I had better get up and start my day. I sat up and the room began to spin. My head started pounding and I lay back down. As I did so, the need to throw up overcame me. I had spoken too soon. I had never felt so sick and nauseated before a race. I was determined to compete. But how?

Very slowly this time, I sat up and began dressing myself and preparing for the press conference. Every jarring action set off a new wave of pressure behind my eyes. I could hardly focus them, and I knew there was no way I could do a race in this condition.

Somehow I made it through the press conference and then quickly retreated to my room to lie down. I forced myself to drink some water, but my head kept pounding. I didn't know how I was going to make it to Trish and Sam's later that afternoon for the pizza party.

After napping for a while, I went to the pizza party, but there was no way I could eat anything. I tried to drink, but that only made me feel more nauseated.

I left the party early and was glad to climb back into my bed. When I woke up on Sunday morning, I felt a little better and was convinced I'd be fit for the race the next day. I just had to win. I was defending my last four wins! Boston was my race, and I didn't want anyone to take it away from me.

I kept a low profile all that day. I still couldn't eat anything substantial, but I did keep a couple of pints of water down. I hoped another good night's rest would help me.

At about two o'clock I rolled over and reached for my Bible, which was on my nightstand. I was in the habit of reading a chapter of Proverbs in line with each day of the month. It was April 16, so I turned to chapter sixteen. I read slowly until I got to verse three. It said, "Commit to the LORD whatever you do, and your plans will succeed." Wow! It hit me between the eyes. Did I really believe it? If I committed my plan to the Lord, would he help me succeed, even with food poisoning? I felt a surge of faith. "Lord," I prayed, "I commit this marathon and my health to you. You say I can win this, and I believe you." A sense of peace came over me. I lay back on the pillow, exhausted from the exertion of reading.

On Monday morning I felt much better. I drank some water and forced down a chocolate energy bar before starting out for the Sheraton Hotel, where the athletes boarded the buses that would transport them to Hopkinton for the start of the race. I pushed to the hotel as I had every year before without any problems.

After the bus dropped us off in Hopkinton, I made my final preparations for the race and began my warmup exercises. I had completed only half of a warmup run when I suddenly felt weak again. *Oh no!* I thought. *This can't be happening.* I tried to stay focused on the race ahead, but it was very difficult. My lightheadedness was back, and the chocolate energy bar was swirling around in my stomach.

When the race started, Louise Sauvage and I got away early. We took turns at pulling. Louise averaged twenty miles per hour, but when it was my turn I could only get up to nineteen miles per hour. This wasn't a good sign so early in the race. At the three-mile mark I was already starting to get weak, and by mile six I knew I was beaten. I began to look for a place where I could pull out of the race without too many media people around. A minute later it hit me: I couldn't pull out, no matter how sick I felt! I had committed this race to God, and I had to give it every bit of energy and talent I possessed. As long as I was conscious, I had to keep stroking. I told myself that if I fainted, that was out of my control. But pulling out for anything less than that would be unacceptable.

I continued to push in Louise's draft. We were still trading pulls with each other at Heartbreak Hill, despite the fact that I had thrown up two times and was so weak I could hardly think straight. I knew I had to get away from Louise on the hill, though, and I prayed out loud. "God, you have to help me here. This is your race!"

I felt a renewed energy as I took my turn in the lead. It was now or never. I stroked as fast as I could, hoping against hope that I was creating a large enough gap to see me through the rest of the race. I threw up once again, but I kept praying and pumping— right up until I broke the finish tape. I had once again broken the course and world records, this time by twenty-eight seconds. Louise was twenty-three seconds behind me. As I listened to "The Star-Spangled Banner" being played, I was in awe of what God had done. There was no earthly way I should have won the race, much less in record-setting time.

It was with a grateful heart that I returned to the White House Rose Garden for more photos with President Clinton.

I continued my winning streak the following year, securing my sixth consecutive win in the Boston Marathon, though for the first time I didn't beat the record I had set the year before. After five years of tailwind, that year there was a crosswind that slowed down the entire field of both able-bodied and wheelchair athletes.

By now, however, I was burned out from the constant stress of training and racing. I decided that I would do one last Boston Marathon in 1996. Winning that would be a great note to retire on. When I broke the news to Marty, he didn't say much. We had always communicated our most emotionally charged thoughts on my training and racing via my training journal. Sure enough, the next morning when I went into the gym, Marty had made an entry in red ink. It read, "I don't have any right to tell you what to do with your life, Jean, but if you quit now you're cutting off an incredible career too early."

I hated to disappoint Marty, but I was adamant. Nine years of professional racing were enough for me. I had to admit I would miss the adrenaline rush and the camaraderie of the athletes, but enough was enough.

Ironically, I got a dose sooner than I expected of what it would be like to be retired. In July 1995, I went houseboating with a large group of friends at a secluded lake on the Kentucky-Tennessee border. On Saturday afternoon, my hostess, Pat, and five others decided to take a speedboat out and go tubing. I went first. The tube had a cover on the bottom so I was able to wedge my legs between the tube and the cover. This kept them from flailing around. Soon we were off. I loved the sensation of skimming over the water. It reminded me of ten years ago when I had first water-skied. I bounced from one side of the wake to the other.

But on one of these bounces I was ejected from the tube. Pat put the boat in neutral and waited for me to climb back in. I was re-wedging my feet between the cover and the tube as I was being pulled along, when I hit the wake from another boat. I heard a crack and signaled for Pat to slow down. I hoped the sound had

just been the tube slapping against my leg. I was looking down to
guide my foot back under the cover when I saw it. My left leg was
at a grotesque forty-five-degree angle. Right away I knew I had
broken my femur.

I signaled for Pat to pull me in.

"What's up?" she asked.

"I've broken my leg," I said, trying hard to hold back tears of
frustration. I couldn't feel anything, but I dreaded what Marty
would say when he found out. How could I have been so careless?

Pat and Kim, a nurse, lifted me into the boat. Kim kept one
hand above the break and one below it. By the time we got to shore
and into my van a big knot of blood had formed around the break.
We raced to the Clay County Hospital in Salina, Tennessee, where
an on-call doctor put my leg in an immobilizer. I wanted my own
doctor to take a look at it before anything more was done, so Pat
drove me home to Champaign.

Dr. Gernant tried to calm me down. "Don't worry, Jean. It will
heal," he said many times as he studied the x-rays. "You have two
choices. One, you can keep your leg in the immobilizer for sixteen
weeks, or two, I can operate and put a pin in your leg, which
would reduce the time in the immobilizer to ten weeks."

I chose the surgery in the hope that I could salvage some of the
remaining racing season. Three weeks later I waved good-bye to the
University of Illinois team as they went off to the National Wheelchair 10-Kilometer Championships. I had won the race the past
three years, and I was saddened by the idea of not competing. It was
hard to be left behind. Yet I was surprised by my reaction. After all,
wasn't I planning to retire for good? Wasn't I going to have to watch

someone else win the Boston Marathon? The thought shocked me, and I realized I wasn't ready to hang up my racing gloves quite yet! Winning was in my blood, and I itched to continue.

My injury was inconvenient for more reasons than just racing. Two weeks before the accident, Alison Davis, a television producer, had committed to creating a one-hour documentary based on my life and sporting achievements. It was to be called *Against the Wind.* Now, I had to start filming with my leg stuck straight out in front of me in an immobilizer!

The making of the documentary compounded the pressure on my already hectic life. I was worried I would lose focus on my racing, so I decided it was time for a new approach. I needed an agent, but not just any agent. I'd had many agents offer me contracts before, but I hadn't been comfortable signing with any of them. I was holding out for an agent who was passionate about wheelchair sports and who understood my Christian faith, since that was the underpinning for so many of the career decisions I now made. I had no idea where to start looking for such a person, or if one even existed. Until I met Maryanna Young. Maryanna was a tall, slender woman with medium brown hair and an air of efficiency. She had first contacted me in her capacity as the cofounder and coordinator of the Idaho Women's Fitness Celebration, a 5-kilometer road race aimed at encouraging women of all types to participate in fitness activities. Maryanna asked me to be the keynote speaker and a competitor in the celebration that year.

When I broke my leg, I called her to say I wouldn't be able to make it to Idaho. She insisted that I come anyway, even though I couldn't race. Her determined attitude made me a little angry. *Who does she think she is?* I thought. *I'm struggling with a broken leg. She should let me out of my commitment.* The last thing I wanted to do was get on an airplane and do any public speaking. I didn't have the slightest idea that one day I'd be glad of Maryanna's tenacity and determination. She wouldn't let me wiggle out of my commitment, so begrudgingly I boarded a plane to Idaho.

On the flight, passengers climbed over my broken leg, which in its immobilized state stuck out into the aisle. By the time we landed in Idaho, I wasn't in a good mood.

Maryanna was waiting for me at the gate, and as soon as she saw me her face fell. "I'm so sorry, Jean," she said. "I wasn't thinking straight. I had no idea it was this awkward for you to travel."

"That's okay. I'm here now," I said, glad that Maryanna finally realized my injury was serious.

The weekend turned out to be less difficult than I thought it would be, and Maryanna made sure I was treated well. On Saturday night, after the event, she came to my hotel room, and we talked for a couple of hours. I found out that Maryanna and I shared a strong Christian faith, which to me was encouraging. As the evening wore on, she said to me, "So, who are your sponsors?"

"Well," I replied, "Eagle Sportschairs in Georgia gives me a new chair and other equipment each year."

"And...?" Maryanna pressed, raising her eyebrows.

"That's it."

She looked me in the eye. "Jean, that's crazy. You're a world-class athlete. You can do much better than that!"

"Yeah, other people have told me that. It's just a matter of getting the right agent," I said.

Maryanna smiled. "What would you think about our working together? I've got some experience in agenting, and I'd love to work with you."

I was speechless. Despite our semi-rocky beginning, I liked Maryanna a lot and had noted she was well respected by everyone involved in planning the event. She'd been tenacious about getting me to Idaho, and I began to think of the good things that could happen if her tenacity were applied to my career development.

"Let's try it!" I said.

Before she left the hotel room, Maryanna and I prayed together, committing this new endeavor to the Lord. We couldn't have imagined how much he would bless it. That day marked the start of a long and very amicable agent-client relationship that was to develop into a friendship.

Just a few months after Maryanna began working with me, she put together a sponsorship proposal for Ocean Spray Cranberries. I had met key executives in this company a year earlier at the Women's Sports Foundation banquet, and I'd been impressed by their innovative programs such as WAVE (Women Athletes Voice of Encouragement) and "Crave to Be Your Best." Both programs elevated the status and profile of many women's sports. In January 1996, I signed my first major corporate sponsorship deal with Ocean Spray. I was proud to be a part of their team.

In July, *Against the Wind* aired on more than four hundred PBS stations. I was pleased with the professional quality of the documentary. When it aired I received many invitations to speak about my disability. I was delighted to explain my view of things to thousands of people. I told them that my disability is a characteristic, like having blond hair or being nearsighted. It's not a defining principle. For example, a person who is nearsighted puts on glasses or contacts in the morning and then goes about his or her regular daily activities. My disability happens to require that I climb into a wheelchair. But once I'm in it, I go about my day hardly ever thinking about my wheelchair.

In 1996, Maryanna accompanied me to Boston. It was a historic year for the Boston Marathon, which was marking its one hundredth running. In 1897 the Boston Athletic Association sponsored its first marathon, which had been inspired by the marathon at the first modern Olympic Games, held in Athens in 1896. The first Boston Marathon had eighteen entrants in the race, all men. The 1996 marathon had a record 38,708 entrants, three times more than the previous year. It seemed as if everyone wanted to play a small part in this significant event.

There were 101 athletes in the wheelchair division, but I had trained hard and I knew I was in top form. I really wanted the trophy for the one hundredth marathon, so I stayed as focused as I could in the days leading up to Patriot's Day and the race, even though I was under enormous pressure to do an endless string of television, newspaper, and radio interviews.

On race day everything went just as I had hoped. Candace Cable, Louise Sauvage, and I stuck together until mile eighteen when I pulled away from them and raced out on my own. I streaked through the finish line in 1:52:56. Not a record, but good enough to secure first place as well as another honor.

At the end of that race, my name was linked for the first time with that of Clarence DeMar. DeMar was a legendary figure who had won the men's open division of the marathon seven times between 1911 and 1930. Unbelievably, DeMar and I were the only two athletes ever to win the race seven times in our divisions. The press immediately posed the question: Could I beat the record and become the first athlete ever to win eight races in Boston?

Winning in 2000.

THIRTEEN

NUMBER EIGHT

I returned to Boston in 1997 determined to be the first athlete ever to win eight Boston Marathons. I was pumped and ready to go. The summer had been great. I'd had many successes, including a silver medal at the 1996 Atlanta Olympic Games and four medals at the Paralympic Games: two gold, a silver, and a bronze.

The trees were still bare when I arrived in Massachusetts ten days early to do some serious workouts up and down the hills in Wompatuck State Park. I was confident in my ability as the best female hill-climber, and I certainly wasn't going near a bowl of clam chowder before this race!

On Patriot's Day, I lined up with Louise Sauvage and Candace Cable, my main competition in the race. After the race began, Louise and I stayed close to each other and at mile two I heard her whisper, "Come on, Jean, let's go."

"Okay," I replied, stroking faster.

Two minutes later we had surged ahead of the others. The two of us raced on together.

We took turns pulling and drafting until mile seventeen, where I decided to test Louise. I stroked forward, trying to open up a gap between us, but she came right with me. *Impressive*, I thought. The only other time she had stuck with me on an uphill stretch was during the race when I had food poisoning. I kept up the pace and eventually a gap opened between us. When we crested the hill, nearly eighteen miles into the race, I had a ten-second lead, but it wasn't enough. On the downward run, Louise closed in on me.

We sped down Chestnut Hill about twenty-two miles into the race and on into Cleveland Circle at twenty miles per hour. There was a left-hand turn at the bottom of the hill, and I knew that if I could get on the inside of Louise, I could come out of the turn in the lead. I hoped I could then push hard and continue to increase the gap between us as I climbed the overpass ahead.

As I got to the bottom of the hill, I steered left and felt my wheel slip into one of the trolley tracks. I had known the tracks were there but had never had a problem crossing them before. *Oh, great! Now I'm going to have to stop and pop my wheel out of the track and Louise will get away from me,* I thought to myself. As I started to do so, *bam!* My wheelchair swung around 180 degrees and crashed sideways onto the pavement, taking me with it since I was strapped tightly into it. It took me a second to realize what had happened. I flipped myself onto my back and began pushing myself up on my elbows as I waited for someone to help get me and my chair upright again.

In an instant, policemen and race volunteers surrounded me, wanting to know how they could help.

"Push down on the front of my chair," I instructed them.

When the chair and I were upright again, I examined my carbon fiber wheels. They weren't broken, but the left tire that was normally glued to the rim had pulled free. I needed to get it back on fast. I could do it myself, but my hands were sweaty inside my gloves and I knew I'd waste valuable seconds getting my gloves on again.

"We have to get the tire back on the rim," I told one man. "You'll need to align the valve with the hole in the rim," I instructed another.

My makeshift pit crew did everything I asked remarkably fast, while I looked up the hill to see if the third-place woman was coming. I knew she couldn't be far behind me.

"What now?" asked a third man.

I looked down. "Get the CO_2 cartridge," I said. "Untape it from my frame. Put it on the tire valve and pull the handle."

I heard the familiar hissing noise, but there was a problem. The air wasn't getting into the tire!

"It's not connected properly," I yelled in a panic. My stomach was in a knot. I could sense the third woman was getting closer.

The men tried over and over to get the cartridge and the valve to connect, but it wouldn't work.

"The cartridge must be defective," I shouted, looking at my Cateye computer. Five minutes had elapsed since the accident. I was on borrowed time. I had to get going, flat tire or not.

"I have to go. I gotta go," I yelled to the crowd that had formed around me.

The crowd parted, and I swung my chair around and pushed off hard. Pushing a wheelchair with a flat tire is as jarring as riding in a car with no suspension. I bumped along, occasionally hopping the front end of my chair to the left to compensate for the flat tire to keep the chair moving in a straight line. At the top of the overpass, I looked back to see someone in a red jersey—Candace Cable! I surged forward. I may have lost first place, but I couldn't let anyone take second from me.

My scraped elbows stung as I sped down Beacon Street, past Kenmore Square and onto Boylston Street. Candace was still twenty-five seconds behind me when I threw my arms up and yelled "Praise God!" at the finish line. The last strains of the Australian national anthem were playing as I wheeled through the finishing chute.

When I came to the end of the chute, the media were waiting. Louise rolled over to me and put her arm around me. "Sorry about the accident," she said, and I knew she meant it. Louise and I were both fierce competitors who liked to win fair and square. Winning because your opponent crashed is an unsatisfying victory. We both knew that I had lost the race more than she had won it this time.

As soon as I finished talking to Louise, the camera crews descended on me. I began to realize I was an even bigger celebrity when I lost than when I won. Camera crews and reporters gathered around me and asked a hundred and one questions about the crash. At one point I looked over at Louise, the race winner, and not a single reporter was focusing on her. I tried to answer the questions in a way that would deflect attention back onto Louise's win rather than my loss.

That night in my hotel room, I flicked through the TV channels and saw the footage of my crash replayed over and over. I began to appreciate how fortunate I'd been to escape with just two grazed elbows. Ten minutes after my crash, one of the male athletes had crashed his racing chair at nearly the same spot, breaking his wrist and keeping him from finishing the race.

Somehow the grace I had tried to exhibit under the pressure of losing "my race" had touched the emotions of the general public. I found out just how much of a role model I had become when, three weeks later, I was back in Boston to speak at a Fellowship of Christian Athletes Banquet. I received a standing ovation before I began speaking!

The following day I traveled to Rhode Island, where another wonderful event awaited me. The University of Rhode Island conferred an honorary doctorate degree on me. After watching friends do endless hours of research and writing and defending dissertations, I thought this was a painless way to get a doctorate.

During the next year, the goal of winning my eighth Boston Marathon never left me. I continued to experiment with my training, averaging one hundred miles of roadwork a week as well as lifting weights three times a week. I reached the point where I could bench press 210 pounds, nearly twice my body weight.

The run up to the 1998 Boston Marathon was one of the most intense times I'd experienced. I was nervous by the time I got to Boston, and even more so after I had run the gauntlet of reporters. They all had the same question: "So, Jean, is this the year you beat Clarence DeMar's record?"

I was glad when race day finally arrived; the pressure was becoming unbearable.

The first half of the race went as usual, with Louise and me breaking away, although a young Swiss athlete named Edith Hunkeler stayed with us until the hills at Newton. When we got there, I broke away from Louise and developed a strong lead. The adrenaline was flowing as I pumped twenty to thirty strokes in a row before taking a break.

As I approached the left turn into Cleveland Circle, I took a couple of extra seconds and applied the brake as I descended the hill. I wanted to have perfect control as I bumped over the trolley tracks where I had crashed the year before. The Boston Athletic Association had also put out orange cones marking a wider turning angle over the tracks. It worked perfectly, and I flew over the tracks, certain I was going to win. I allowed myself a backward glance. "Yes!" I yelled. Louise was more than one hundred meters behind me!

As I saw the finish tape, I let up and prepared to raise my arms in victory.

At mile twenty-five I felt the muscles in my forearms tighten up and my hands began to cramp. I could feel Louise closing in on me, but my arms weren't responding. I coasted for a few seconds while I ripped the Velcro on my gloves apart, opening my hand to increase circulation. I closed the glove again, this time more loosely, and continued racing toward Boylston Street. I glanced behind me. Louise was gaining on me, but I didn't think she could catch me in the half-mile that remained. I punched my wheels as hard as I could, visualizing myself with the laurel wreath on my head and the winner's trophy in my hands.

Only fifty meters to go! The finish line loomed in front of me. I heard the public address announcer yell, "And here comes Jean Driscoll, eight-time winner of the Boston Marathon!" The crowd of thirty thousand spectators cheered boisterously. A group started yelling "Jean, Jean, the Boston Queen!" I couldn't wait to cut that tape. Relief flooded through me. I knew Louise was close, but obviously not close enough. As I saw the finish line tape, I let up and prepared to raise my arms in victory. As I did so, whoosh! Louise Sauvage flew past me and cut the tape first!

Everything went silent, totally silent. My mouth gaped open. I tried to comprehend what had just happened. Was it real? Had Louise really cut the tape? I stopped my chair, grabbed the steering bar and put my head down. My body and my mind were numb. *What just happened?* I asked myself again and again.

The announcer regained his composure. "We need to check the results here, but it appears that Jean Driscoll has not won the race as first announced. Louise Sauvage appears to be our 1998 winner."

I could hear Louise screaming and yelling, "I did it. I never gave up!"

As she turned around to go back to the awards platform, Louise stopped next to me for a moment. She put her arms around me, and I hugged her back. "Congratulations," I said. I tried to be as gracious on the outside as I could, though inside I was torn apart and dazed, still wondering how it could have happened.

Later that day, the public address announcer came up to me. "Jean," he said in a desperate voice. "I'm so sorry I called you the winner early. I blew it. I thought the chair coming up beside you was one of the guys. Everyone did. I thought you were the only woman on Boylston and you had it in the bag. I was shocked when I realized the blue chair was Louise's. I had no idea."

He looked so upset that I ended up comforting him. "It's okay. Mistakes happen." I knew that if I had been aware that Louise was so close I would not have stopped sprinting. I would have pumped right through the finish line. *But that's racing,* I told myself, knowing that ultimately I was responsible for the outcome, not the announcer.

As it happened, it was the closest finish in the history of the Boston Marathon. Louise beat me by an estimated two-tenths of a second. Because marathon clocks don't go to hundredths of a second, we were credited with the identical time of 1:41:19, though her name appeared above mine on the official list of winners.

Our finish became CNN's "Play of the Day," and newspaper headlines declared, "Driscoll Comes Up Short" and "Sauvage Reigning Queen of Boston."

Over the next few days, I tried to process my defeat. It was so different from the loss the year before when disaster struck and it became obvious I could not win. But this year I was beaten fair and square. I analyzed every mile of the race over and over, picking out many places where I could have made up a second here and a second there, wiping away the split-second difference between winning and losing.

Following my loss, I was amazed by how the media talked about my graciousness in the face of defeat. What graciousness? I wasn't feeling gracious. I believed in good sportsmanship, but inside I was torn up. Still, I promised everyone that next year I would be back. I still wanted to be the first person in the history of the Boston Marathon to win eight times. But could I? I began to wonder if my winning days were over. Had my athletic abilities peaked? Was finishing second the best I was now capable of?

I decided I should probably consider retiring, but I couldn't find any peace with that decision—not until I tried at least one more Boston Marathon!

The 1999 marathon was held on April 19. I was in good shape and was ready to regain my title. Louise Sauvage was also there at the starting line, and she looked well rested. I sensed it was going to be a close race, though I hoped my superior hill-climbing ability would make the difference. Once the race began, Louise and I quickly pulled away from the pack. In front of us was a Swedish woman who pushed hard during the first half of the course and maintained at least a thirty-second lead. She had never raced in the Boston Marathon before, however, and didn't save enough strength for the hills that awaited us on the second half of the course. Louise and I quickly passed her as we entered Newton. We then began a nerve-wracking game of cat-and-mouse. I would get the lead on Louise, and she would come right back at me. As I hoped, I opened up a gap on her on the hills, but not quite enough to stay ahead of her on the downhill stretches and on the flat.

As we rolled onto Boylston Street, Louise was in front with me in her draft. I pushed for all I was worth, but I couldn't pass her in the final sprint. We zoomed across the finish line with the identical times of 1:42:23, but Louise was marginally ahead and was declared the winner. Once again I had been beaten, and Louise was now a three-time winner. I congratulated her for winning a tough race and rolled through the chutes to talk to Marty Morse while Louise was surrounded by camera crews and reporters.

It took a long time to adjust to losing that race. I had been so close, and I had given it my all. Again I asked myself if it was time to retire. Once again I came to the same conclusion. There had to be one more Boston Marathon trophy out there with my name on it, and I was determined to claim it!

That year I went on to win my eleventh consecutive Bloomsday race in Spokane, Washington, and while there I was persuaded to participate in one of the most grueling races in the world. The Midnite Sun Wheelchair Challenge went from Fairbanks to Anchorage, Alaska. I knew the 367-mile race would give me the endurance I needed to carry me into the next marathon season. The event was set up so that wheelchair racers and handcyclists (those who use geared bikes that are powered by arms rather than legs) competed in separate divisions but completed the same course. Every day for nine days, we would race between thirty-eight and forty-six miles.

Each race participant had a support crew of three people: one to drive a camper to sleep in during the event, and two to drive behind the athlete during the race, carrying spare parts and other supplies that might be needed. The support crews also served to protect the racers from dangerous wildlife, like bears and moose!

From the moment we set out in Fairbanks, I knew I was in for the most difficult race of my life. Freezing rain chilled me to the bone, and on day three a thirty-mile-per-hour headwind slowed us all down. Sometimes it gusted to sixty miles per hour, causing me to push down hills at only five to eight miles per hour when normally they could have been negotiated at forty-five miles per hour. On one occasion I stopped pushing on a downhill stretch and the wind actually blew me backward!

I started the race with the goal of beating the women's record time, but I quickly adjusted my expectations to merely finishing. By the time we got to Anchorage, the other female athlete in the race had dropped out, making me the only woman to finish.

The Midnite Sun Wheelchair Challenge went from Fairbanks to Anchorage, Alaska.

Even though I didn't set a record to end the century, I did receive another honor. *Sports Illustrated for Women* chose me as one of the top one hundred female athletes of the twentieth century. In fact, I was named in the top twenty-five, along with Olympic gold medalists Jackie Joyner-Kersee and Bonnie Blair, tennis champs Chris Everett and Billy-Jean King, and soccer phenomenon Mia Hamm. I was stunned at being recognized with this legendary group of women.

As I flipped through the pages of the magazine, I couldn't help wondering if some of my old school friends would see my name. I smiled as I thought of their reactions. It would seem impossible to them, just as it would have looked that way to me as a child. Without a doubt, anyone from my grade school or high school would have identified me as the person *least likely* to be named one of the top athletes of the century. I had come a long way since those days. Rather than being known for my disability and the things I couldn't do, it felt good to be known for what I could do and do well.

As the 2000 Boston Marathon drew near, I was more confident in my preparation than I had been in the last few years. I had gone back to my training journals and looked up how I'd trained in the mid-1990s when I was on my winning streak. I found that I'd done more strength endurance weight training back then and adjusted my training schedule so that I was doing more sets and repetitions of lifting exercises at a lower weight. I had also averaged between 100 and 120 miles a week on the road. In the last few years during my training I had either been way above or way below that figure. I had done a lot of wind work back in the nineties, following a circuit from the university and back. That way I got to push against the wind as well as have it at my back. I returned to this format instead of concentrating on the point-to-point training I'd been doing. (Using this approach, I had trained with a tailwind and would go up to twenty-three miles at a time. I would then be picked up in a van and brought back to the university.)

I arrived in Boston five days early. In addition to Ocean Spray, I had the logos of three new corporate sponsors to wear on my jersey this year. The sponsors were Litehouse, AccessLife.com, and California Dates, and I was determined to represent them as best I could. After the press conference on Thursday morning, I drove out to Wompatuck State Park to test myself on the hills.

Everything leading up to the race was similar to the years

before. Sam and Trish, Marty's brother and sister-in-law, hosted another wonderful pizza party for me and some of the other University of Illinois athletes. The next day my team of supporters, which included friends and business acquaintances, and I went to lunch at a southwestern restaurant. I was feeling peaceful and confident in my training for the race. I knew I was as strong as I had ever been on the hills, and I was pushing well on the flats too. However, I was also well aware that I had lost the last three marathons. I knew this would be a defining race for me. If I lost the 2000 Boston Marathon I wasn't sure I would have the fire in my belly to come back for another try.

When I woke at six o'clock on Monday morning, the first thing I did was flick on the Weather Channel. It reported that a headwind gusting up to twenty-five miles per hour was expected for the race. "Well," I told myself as I munched some dry Cheerios and downed them with cold water, "no one will be setting any records today, but I've done my share of wind work. I'm ready to go!"

As my friends and I made our way to the Sheraton from the hotel where we were staying, many people wished me good luck. I was so glad to be back in Boston. The city had the best spectators in the world.

When we got to the Sheraton, I decided to be on the last bus pulling out. That way I would have less time to be harassed by reporters at the other end. This proved to be a nerve-wracking choice.

We had gone about five miles in the bus when smoke began to pour out of the exhaust pipe. The driver pulled over and stepped outside. From my seat on the right side I could see him talking with another employee from the Massachusetts Transit Authority, who had been driving behind us. Eventually they decided the bus needed more oil and the driver poured a couple of pints into the engine.

We pulled back onto the road, but just as we arrived at a toll plaza, the same thing happened again. There was another conference, and more oil was poured into the failing engine.

"We tried to get another bus to pick you up," the driver told us gravely as he climbed back on board. "But there's nothing available. We'll just have to hope we make it."

Normally this kind of a disruption so close to race time would have disturbed me greatly, but this time my peaceful confidence stayed with me as the bus edged its way to Hopkinton. We arrived at the elementary school where we would get ready for the race only fifteen minutes behind schedule. I managed to elude the reporters and slip into the sanctuary of the school gym before a microphone could be stuck in my face.

I was given Number 102 for the race. I taped the number to my helmet, and also pinned it to my knees and the back of my chair.

At 11:40 A.M., I was sitting at the starting line alongside my nemesis, Louise Sauvage. In a customary salute we bumped gloves and said "safe race" to each other.

I looked up and Guy Morse, the race director, caught my eye. He smiled and nodded at me, as if to say, "This is your year, Jean!" I smiled back, hoping to see him again on the winner's podium.

The starter's gun fired at 11:45, and we began the paced section of the race as usual. Half a mile later, when the pace car sped away, four of us came together to form the lead pack. The group consisted of Miriam Nibley, a student who rents a room in my home, a Canadian named Chantal Petitclerc, Louise Sauvage, and me. Chantal stayed with us until the five-mile mark, then she dropped back.

Miriam stayed with us for three more miles before yelling, "Go for it, Jean!" as I pulled out ahead of her. She soon faded out of sight.

It was down to Louise and me, and we battled neck and neck for the rest of the race. As usual, I was better on the uphill climbs while she gained ground on the downhill stretches.

I could see the finish line, and I raced toward it.

We went back and forth, trading places as we each took a pull. It was tough work racing into a headwind. I was pulling at about fourteen miles per hour, but when Louise got in front sometimes she purposely slowed it down to thirteen miles per hour.

"Come on, Louise, take a fair pull!" I finally yelled at her, frustrated that she was slowing down and saving herself for the hill climbs. She eventually sped up, and we raced along together.

We stayed together until Heartbreak Hill, where I used my superior hill-climbing ability to open up a gap on her.

About halfway up the grueling climb, I turned my head and looked back. Louise was about twenty meters behind me, but she was not giving up. Determination was etched into her face. I couldn't slacken my pace one bit.

I crested the hill in the lead, but on the downhill, Louise began to catch up. I pushed my wheels faster and harder than I ever had, and with the extra effort I managed to keep Louise at bay. I turned onto Boylston Street still in the lead and looked back again. All I could see was the orange snow fence, marking the route and holding back the spectators. Adrenaline surged through me. I could see the finish line, and I raced toward it, unwilling to stop pushing until I felt the tape break across my chest.

The crowd roared wildly and I heard the public address announcer yell, "She's done it! Number eight! Jean Driscoll, eight-time winner of the Boston Marathon!" As he uttered the words, I felt the finish tape burst in two. I raised my arms. This time I had done it. "Praise God!" I yelled.

I wheeled through the chute to a standing ovation from the Boston Athletic Association officials and the finish-line volunteers. Many of them had tears in their eyes as they gave me a thumbs-up and cheered me on. Guy Morse, the race director, engulfed me in a bear hug. "I'm so excited for you!" he beamed. "I was hoping you'd do well!"

I wheeled myself up to the winners' platform. I had a huge grin fixed to my face and I was far too happy to cry.

Frank Porter, president of the Boston Athletic Association, welcomed me onto the platform. He leaned down and spoke in my ear. "You're the only American who's going to win today, and this is the only time we're going to hear our national anthem played. Thank you!"

As the music started, I put my hand on my heart and sang along. When it was over, cameras and reporters surrounded me. Larry Rawson from ESPN threw the first question, "So, where have you been?"

"I don't know," I replied, "but it sure feels great to be back!"

And it did, not only for myself, but for all those who were there with me. When everything had settled down, I went back to the hotel for a break before the awards ceremony. Waiting there for me in my room were so many people I loved. There were my mom and dad and my brother Ray, who had come out to support me. There were also Maryanna Young, my agent, and Mary McGovern, the woman responsible for encouraging Ocean Spray to consider sponsoring me. Sarah, Lynn, and Laurie, three of my dear friends from church were there as well, along with Miriam Nibley, who had finished third in the race. As usual, five or six members of Marty's family were there along with several business acquaintances.

As we celebrated, there was a knock at the door. Sarah opened it, and in walked a room service waiter wheeling a trolley piled high with hors d'oeuvres and sparkling cider. "Compliments of the Fairmont Copley Plaza Hotel to help celebrate your eighth win," he said with a smile.

"Thank you," I said, touched by the gesture, though I didn't need anything more to help me celebrate. I had everything I'd ever wanted right there in the hotel room, and my eighth Boston victory besides.

Dr. Driscoll?!

My parents help me enjoy the pavilion named in my honor.

Epilogue

The days since the 104th running of the Boston Marathon and my eighth win have turned into months, but I am still smiling. The experience will serve as a landmark for the rest of my life. I do have other goals and other dreams, however. I am constantly challenged by the very advice I give to other people: "Dream big and work hard." It's risky to dream big, and hard work requires sacrifices. The journey toward any goal will stretch you at times, but it has the potential to change your perspective on and enjoyment of life in lasting ways.

I believe the biggest limitations we have are the ones we place on ourselves or the ones we allow others to place on us. Once you realize that, you're halfway over the barrier in front of you. As a child, I placed many limitations on myself. As an adult, I had people come into my life who wouldn't let me do that. I thank the Lord for those people!

It is true that very few people make an Olympic team, sing the national anthem at the Super Bowl, fly to the moon, enjoy life as a movie star, engage in sports at a professional level, become president of the United States, write a bestseller, have a garden like

Martha Stewart, or lead a ministry like Billy Graham. But there *are* people who do these things. You can be one of them. I once heard Jackie Joyner-Kersee speak at a banquet to some young girls in the audience and she told them, "Don't follow in my footsteps. You make your own footsteps." I love that! It's good advice for all of us. Dream big, work hard, and make the footsteps that will lead you toward joy and purpose in your life.

For further information, contact the nonprofit organization, *Determined to Win,* at P.O. Box 1038, Champaign, IL 61824-1038 or call (888) 440-0417. Also see the Web site *www.jeandriscoll.com.*

Milestones in My Life

Date	Age	Significant Event(s)
November 18, 1966		Born (with spina bifida and cleft palate)
May 1968	18 mo.	Twin brothers born (Ray and Ron). My sister, Frances, is two and a half years old
September 1971	4	Started kindergarten
January 1972	5	Youngest brother born (Jacques)
1975	8	First broken leg, third grade, first Easter Seals two-week summer camp
1976	9	Easter Seals Poster Child, fourth grade, learned to ride a two-wheeled bike
Summer 1979	12	First thirteen-mile bike ride (on a single-speed bike) to Aunt Joan's
Winter 1979	13	Won ten-speed bike in read-a-thon for multiple sclerosis, eighth grade

Date	Age	Significant Event(s)
Summer 1980	13	Biked thirteen miles (on ten speed) to Aunt Joan's with friend, Dawn
August 1980	13	Started high school at Divine Savior Holy Angels (all-girl school)
November 1980		Bike accident (six days before my fourteenth birthday)
November 1980-November 1981	14	Five hip operations, spent year in a body cast, made friends with nurses
December 1981	15	Became owner of first wheelchair after left hip began dislocating again
January 1982	15	Returned to high school for two weeks (second semester, tenth grade)
February 1982	15	Surgery on first pressure sore
June 1982	15	Surgery on second pressure sore
September 1982	15	Transferred to Custer High School for junior and senior years
May 1983	16	First exposed to wheelchair sports
April 1984	17	Surgery to implant artificial sphincter
June 1984	17	Graduated from high school
August 1984	17	Began classes at University of Wisconsin, Milwaukee, in nursing
Summer 1985	18	Received driver's license, bought first sportschair

Date	Age	Significant Event(s)
January 1986	19	Flunked out of college, surgery on third pressure sore
January–December 1986	19	Worked as live-in mother's helper for former nurse (Lori O'Brien)
April 1986	19	Met Brad Hedrick, who recruited me to attend the University of Illinois
May 1986	19	Attended first wheelchair track meet
August 1986	19	Found first sponsor, Jim Derse, who bought first racing chair and airline ticket
November 1986	19	Flew to Phoenix, Ariz., for first road race
April 1987	20	Began working with racing and swimming coaches, Don and Mikel Vandello
May 1987	20	Competed in regional track meet, qualified for nationals (in swimming too)
June 1987	20	Competed at Nationals in Houston and won all five of my track events, had to forgo swimming competition because the races were held at the same time, qualified for U.S. Developmental Track Team going to England (Derse Foundation paid for me to go)

Date	Age	Significant Event(s)
July 1987	20	Competed in Aylesbury, England, and won nine gold medals
August 1987	20	Moved to Champaign, Ill., began studies in speech communication and became a dual sport athlete: wheelchair basketball and track
August 1988	21	First attempt at qualifying for Olympic Wheelchair Exhibition Event; failed to make it, but I did qualify for the Paralympic Team
October 1988	21	First Paralympic Games in Seoul, South Korea, won four medals: one gold (4x200m relay), one silver (4x100m relay), two bronze (200m and 400m events)
May 1989	22	First national-level victory in a road race, Bloomsday-Spokane, WA
October 1989	22	First marathon (Chicago), finished second and qualified for Boston
March 1990	23	Second marathon (L.A.), borrowed teammate's chair, miserable race
April 1990	23	University of Illinois women's wheelchair basketball team wins national championship
April 1990	23	Entered first Boston Marathon, won and broke the world record by nearly seven minutes

Date	Age	Significant Event(s)
July 1990	23	Competed in Goodwill Games (Seattle) and broke the world record in 1,500-meter track event
January 1991	24	Finished B.A. with honors and began M.S. in rehabilitation administration
April 1991	24	University of Illinois women's wheelchair basketball team wins national championship for second year; this is my last season of basketball
April 1991	24	Competed in second Boston Marathon and broke the world record again
August 17, 1991	24	Jean Driscoll Day proclaimed by Governor Tommy Thompson in state of Wisconsin
October 1991	24	Named Women's Sports Foundation's Amateur Sportswoman of the Year
February 7, 1992	25	Jean Driscoll Day proclaimed by Mayor Jeffrey Markland of Urbana, Ill., and Mayor Dannel McCollum of Champaign, Ill.
April 1992	25	Sang national anthem at Milwaukee Brewers home opener
April 1992	25	Third Boston victory, third world record

Date	Age	Significant Event(s)
June 1992	25	Committed my life to Christ
August 1992	25	First Olympic Team, 800m Wheelchair Exhibition Event, silver medal, Barcelona, Spain
August 1992	25	Second Paralympic Team, one gold medal (4x100m relay), Barcelona, Spain
January 1993	26	Finished M.S. in rehabilitation administration
April 1993	26	Fourth consecutive Boston victory, fourth world record
April 1994	27	Fifth Boston victory, fifth world record, despite food poisoning
July 1994	27	Broke world record in 10,000m track event, World Track Championships in Berlin, Germany
April 1995	28	Sixth Boston victory, no world record for the first time
July 1995	28	Broke left femur while tubing behind a boat
August 1995	28	Surgery to implant pin in broken femur
September 1995	28	Began working with agent, Maryanna Young
January 1996	29	Signed first major endorsement contract with Ocean Spray Cranberries, Inc.

Date	Age	Significant Event(s)
April 1996	29	Seventh consecutive Boston victory (100th running of Boston Marathon)
August 1996	29	Second Olympic Team, 800m Wheelchair Exhibition Event, silver medal, Atlanta, Ga.
August 1996	29	Third Paralympic Team, two gold medals (10,000m—broke world record, marathon), one silver (5000m), and one bronze (1500m) Atlanta, Ga.
April 1997	30	First loss at Boston, crashed at mile 22 on trolley tracks
May 1997	30	Received honorary doctorate (Humane Letters and Sciences) University of Rhode Island
April 1998	31	Second loss at Boston (by .2 seconds)
April 1999	32	Third loss at Boston (by .5 seconds)
October 1999	32	Signed second major endorsement contract with Litehouse Foods
December 1999	33	Named Number 25 on Sports Illustrated for Women Top 100 Female Athletes of the Century
February 2000	33	Signed third major endorsement contract with AccessLife.com

Date	Age	Significant Event(s)
March 2000	33	Won L.A. Marathon for the third time
March 2000	33	Signed fourth endorsement contract with California Dates
April 2000	33	Won a record-breaking eighth Boston Marathon